QUEER SLASHERS

ICONS OF HORROR

Marc Olivier, series editor

QUEER SLASHERS

PETER MARRA

INDIANA UNIVERSITY PRESS

This book is a publication of

Indiana University Press
Herman B Wells Library 350
1320 East 10th Street
Bloomington, Indiana 47405 USA

iupress.org

First Printing 2025

Library of Congress Cataloging-in-Publication Data

Names: Marra, Peter (Professor), author.
Title: Queer slashers / Peter Marra.
Description: Bloomington, Indiana : Indiana University Press, 2025. |
  Series: Icons of horror | Includes bibliographical references and index.
Identifiers: LCCN 2024045562 (print) | LCCN 2024045563 (ebook) | ISBN
  9780253071934 (hardback) | ISBN 9780253071934 (paperback) | ISBN
  9780253071965 (ebook)
Subjects: LCSH: Slasher films—History and criticism. | Queer theory. |
  Horror films—History and criticism. | LCGFT: Film criticism.
Classification: LCC PN1995.9.S554 M37 2025 (print) | LCC PN1995.9.S554
  (ebook) | DDC 791.43/6164—dc23/eng/20241023
LC record available at https://lccn.loc.gov/2024045562
LC ebook record available at https://lccn.loc.gov/2024045563

Cover image courtesy of Anna Paddock @vorbees.

Dedicated to Ivor Novello, Laird Cregar, Farley Granger,
Vincent Price, Anthony Perkins, Victor Buono, Sal Mineo,
Tab Hunter, Divine, Mark Patton, Peaches Christ,
and all the queer slashers.

CONTENTS

QUEER SLASHERS

INTRODUCTION

ANTHONY PERKINS LOWERING A KNIFE, dressed as Mother in *Psycho* (Alfred Hitchcock, 1960). Beefcake Sal Mineo lifting weights and then murdering Elaine Stritch (how gay!) in *Who Killed Teddy Bear* (Joseph Cates, 1965). Late-career Tab Hunter as a sexually impotent killer in the Roger Corman B movie *Sweet Kill* (Curtis Hanson, 1973), later retitled *The Arousers*. Victor Buono, a burly femme, leaving baby dolls behind at the scenes of his murders in *The Strangler* (Burt Topper, 1964). Farley Granger as an erotically charged Leopold and Loeb style killer in *Rope* (Alfred Hitchcock, 1948) and as a spurned World War II veteran who terrorizes a high school graduation dance in *The Prowler* (Joseph Zito, 1981). Ivor Novello *and* Laird Cregar both as dangerous strangers in *The Lodger* almost two decades apart (Alfred Hitchcock, 1927, and John Brahm, 1944). Vincent Price in . . . well, just about everything. Queer performers have often been the face of murder in cinematic horror, their screen presence leaned on and exploited to convey a sense of difference, which cinema has continually rewritten as a form of danger. Queer people are not historically known for their violence or menace and, contrarily, have been among the most vulnerable to discrimination and physical harm. So, why us? How did the victims of so much

1

tangible violence become cinema's perfect killers? Perhaps more devastatingly, what is the cost of this history to us, and what can we do in the present with this lineage of queer killers, knowing that our cinematic past can never be undone?

The documentary *Scream, Queen! My Nightmare on Elm Street* (Roman Chimienti and Tyler Jensen, 2019) explores the legacy of this queer association with media violence for one specific actor: Mark Patton, star of *A Nightmare on Elm Street 2: Freddy's Revenge* (Jack Sholder, 1985). Though he is now publicly out as gay and HIV+, Patton was at that time a closeted and very scared young actor trying to prove himself a leading man amid the reignited queerphobic panic of the 1980s AIDS epidemic. *Elm Street 2* opened in theaters about one month after the tragic death of gay actor Rock Hudson, who became a landmark celebrity case for public awareness of HIV/AIDS in his final years. Upon the film's release, speculation about its queer themes fueled backlash that caused Patton to flee from the public eye despite the promise of a major movie career.

Elm Street 2 utilized a possession narrative rather than a straight slasher approach, and this shift emphasized subtext about adolescent boys questioning their heterosexuality. In the film, Freddy Krueger (Robert Englund) doesn't want to kill the protagonist, Jesse (Patton), in his dreams (as he did the victims of the first film) but instead hopes to enter the waking world through Jesse's body. This leads to a series of exchanges where Jesse speaks about his fear of Freddy Krueger being "inside" him, which make up some of the movie's juiciest moments of queer-soaked double meaning. Another once-maligned but now celebrated moment of queer display is a scene where Jesse dances around his bedroom and lip-synchs to the disco song "Touch Me" by Fonda Rae. This includes a shot of him bumping his dresser drawer closed with his denim-clad ass and a relatable instance of embarrassment when his mother walks in on him as he shoots a very phallic-looking pop gun held directly above his thrusting crotch. Harry

Fig 0.1 Jesse in *A Nightmare on Elm Street 2: Freddy's Revenge* (1985) booty-bumping his dresser drawer closed as was scripted and emphasized with a close-up shot.

Benshoff, in *Monsters in the Closet*, his study of homosexuality in horror films, reads *Elm Street 2* in the context of the AIDS crisis as speaking to common heterosexual fears at the time of queer men as contagious, both in the sense of transmitting HIV and in recruiting young children into queer lives.[1]

The documentary *Scream, Queen!* is framed as an investigation into the relationship between the exploited queer screen presence of Mark Patton and the film's predominantly straight creative team. While Patton became viscerally aware that the film was playing with queer themes during production and suffered the greatest public backlash upon the film's release, its straight writer and director deferred or outright denied decisions to play on Patton's queerness and were able to consistently evade responsibility.[2] Director Jack Sholder claims throughout the documentary to have never perceived any such themes during production, and in a 2007 interview, screenwriter David Chaskin identified Patton as the primary cause for the film's queer meanings. He conceded an intention in his script to play on the homophobic fears of the film's target demographic of adolescent boys by insinuating that Jesse questions his sexuality before ultimately learning to control "his latent homosexuality" through "the love of a good woman."[3] However, according to Chaskin, Patton's casting over-amplified this intended subtext. He is quoted as saying, "There were certain choices that were made (e.g., casting) that, I think, pushed the subtext to a higher level and stripped away whatever subtlety there may have been."[4] Chaskin acknowledges Sholder's denial that he understood any such subtext and concludes that it must have happened through "osmosis."[5] There's a lot to unpack there. For the purposes of this book, the thing I most want to emphasize is this central problem in which "osmosis," or some ambient understanding of queer potential, works at once through the straight creatives who helmed the film and against the queer actor who was its star.

Elm Street 2 provides us with a potent example of queerness's seeming omnipresence yet invisibility from public discourse. *Scream, Queen!* helpfully stages a reparative intervention that challenges this contradiction from the vantage point of contemporary queer life. It reaches into a past where queer people were omitted from mainstream horror's surface representations and asks its makers to admit that we were always there, and they knew it. During one scene of the documentary, at a reunion of the cast and crew of *Elm Street 2*, director Jack Sholder comments on some of the more loaded queer moments in the film. He addresses a scene in which Jesse follows his high school PE teacher (Marshall Bell) into what appears to be a queer leather bar and then into the locker room showers, where Krueger strips the coach naked and whips his bare ass with a towel. Sholder remarks he had no idea the scene might come across as gay. He is reminded by cast and crew that they did, in fact, scout and shoot at a prominent gay bar. He comments that sure, this happened, but none of the regular patrons were there during that process. So, he didn't really know it was a gay bar. He is next reminded that the script specified this to be a "transvestite bar," and casting took note of this when hiring background performers. The haze of verbal ambiguity falls slowly away and reveals that perhaps, beneath the applied cultural fog, everyone making the movie knew, on some level, exactly what they were doing—although perhaps they never talked about it, not in precise terms. It happened, as Chaskin suggests, through "osmosis."

A helpful way to understand circumstances such as this is by considering Eve Kosofsky Sedgwick's explanation of "homosexual panic," a legal defense in which an attacker cites their fear of the victim's homosexuality as justification for their violent attack. Sedgwick raises the question of how the meaning of "homosexual" in this altercation can be seen as accounting for both the attacker's fear of being implicated as queer and the specific punitive actions taken against the person who suffers violence for being gay. Sedgwick argues for an understanding of queerness as a set of overlapping universalizing and minoritizing discourses. She uses this complex structure to verbalize how all people, including straight people, are implicated in queerness, and yet simultaneously, queer people uniquely suffer for it.[6] Sedgwick contends that in order for the "homosexual panic" legal defense to make sense, there must be some societal belief that the attacker is made to question their own sexuality when approached by a gay man. A jury must see the excuse that the attacker felt threatened by the gay man's sexuality as logical. They must relate to this experience so strongly as to imagine they might react similarly. This is not the case in circumstances of race, religion, etc. No one who commits hate crimes against other minority groups speaks of feeling as though they were made to question their own identity in this encounter. Yet in instances of queer bashing, defendants have successfully made a case for their panic. By Sedgwick's account, minoritizing discourses speak of the way we see *queer* and *gay* as terms that describe a distinct sexual minority. In the case of "homosexual panic" defenses, the minoritized person would be the victim of violence who is understood to be gay. The attacker, the jury, and the justice system, however, acknowledge universalizing discourses in their acquittal as they see panic, or self-investigation by the attacker, as an acceptable reason to feel threatened. As if queer could happen to everyone, even you. In the case of *Elm Street 2*, it seems that Chaskin, Sholder, and the rest of the film's straight creatives participated within the queer meanings of the film from a universalizing stance wherein straight people can see and explore themselves through a self-interrogating encounter with queerness. Chaskin's account of how he hoped the film might play on adolescent boys' fears about questioning their sexuality specifically recognizes this potential for a straight audience to investigate fears about their own sexuality during an encounter with queer possibilities. Yet it was Patton, a gay man, who was implicated as a queer minority and therefore imagined to be somehow more culpable in arousing the film's queer meanings. In a way, Patton's entire experience amounts to a very public form of "homosexual panic" in which the film's straight creatives and audiences felt threatened by how the film made them feel and what questions about themselves it raised, and therefore attempted to isolate the polymorphous meanings of this cinematic encounter to Patton's own allegedly insuppressible gayness.

Queer studies of horror have previously framed the genre in terms of both its universalizing potential to situate all viewers, queer and straight, within a queer vantage point and its overlapping minoritizing appeal for queer audiences. Alexander Doty describes how "the central conventions of horror . . . actually encourage queer positioning" and, consequently, how "everyone's pleasure in [horror] is 'perverse,' is queer, as much of it takes place within the space of the contra-heterosexual and the contra-straight."[7] Doty's take on the queerness of horror is twofold: that there is a unique space for queer readings of horror because of its violent distortions of heterosexuality, normative gender roles, etc., and that horror is also universally queer, that it positions

Fig 0.2 Actor Mark Patton confronting screenwriter David Chaskin about his remarks blaming Patton's casting for making the film too gay in *Scream, Queen! My Nightmare on Elm Street* (2019).

everyone queerly. Harry Benshoff interprets the allegorical qualities of the horror film as expressions of outsider perspectives that appeal to a queerly positioned spectator. Benshoff determines that "horror stories and monster movies, perhaps more than any other genre, actively invoke queer readings, because of their obvious metaphorical (non-realist) forms and narrative formats which disrupt the heterosexual status quo."[8] Like Doty, Benshoff also identifies a place for both straight and queer audiences in this practice. He likens the experience of horror to Bakhtin's formulation of Carnival in which there are strict time parameters binding a finite celebration of deviance. However, queer viewers, he states, are more likely not to return from this place of deviance. Rather, they live there. Speaking of the particularly important role of the queer viewer in this practice, Benshoff states that "the cinematic monster's subjective position is more readily acceded to by a queer viewer—someone who already situates him/herself outside a patriarchal, heterosexist order and the popular culture texts that it produces"[9] Collectively, these accounts of both queer and *queered* horror spectatorship adapt elements of Sedgwick's universalizing and minoritizing discourses as they account for the ways in which all who watch horror may enjoy the queer address of the genre, yet queer spectators may find the genre especially potent because of their lived experiences.

Though queer and straight audiences may both achieve an unexpected allegiance with cinematic killers when positioned queerly by horror films, there is also potential to think about how queer audiences may experience a painful paradox like Patton and other on-screen queer talent. We may feel that we are a part of a universally queer engagement with cinema in the theaters and other venues we share with straight audiences watching these films. And yet, when we leave the theater, there are ramifications for us in real life that do not apply to them. We must contend with the ongoing mythology of queer men as sexual predators of children, of trans women as dangers in public spaces such as bathrooms and locker rooms. The queer cinematic killer speaks the inverse of reality, which is that queer people have historically been the targets of legislative discrimination and physical violence rather than aggressors. Ultimately, *Scream, Queen!* documents the dismal failure of *Elm Street 2*'s straight director and screenwriter to understand the minoritizing blame for the queerness of their film that was placed on the shoulders of Mark Patton. It also conveys that though they were able to attune themselves to a universalized sense of queerness well enough to convey the film's queer meanings, these straight filmmakers ultimately escaped all minoritizing blame. They did not share in Patton's experience of being a scared closeted young actor, of having a lover sick with HIV and then contracting the virus, of being made the face of this "gay movie" that was mocked and ridiculed by homophobic fans.

As a queer horror viewer watching *Scream, Queen!*, I related tremendously to Patton. One reason for this was that we both shared a simple wish at one time or another for straight filmmakers to affirm their role in fashioning a connection between horror movies and our queer lives. I wrote a dissertation on slasher movies and how they could be queer and radical, but I found myself struggling to defend a set of films for which I felt both affection and reservation. I read interviews with writers and directors, searching for some trace of allyship, of knowing their transgressive killers might speak positively to queer audiences' understandings of their own power. I found very little evidence. As a result, I lost the will to make a case for these films as important queer works. In time, I realized that instead, I wanted to help popularize the queer voices who have taken the form of the slasher and made it into something new. We as queer people are so often made to explain our interest in straight media, but truly queer cinema remains often invisibly niche. We are cornered into arguments about whether mainstream horror is or isn't queer, what was intended or not intended, or if that even matters. Yet our films, the ones made for and by our communities, receive comparably far less attention in all arenas: popular media, academia, horror conventions, etc. For those reasons, in this book I will be speaking about the canonical slasher of the 1970s and '80s as a foundational set of texts through which to better understand the subsequent impact of queer slashers, meaning slasher films made by queer writers and directors. In doing so, I hope to transform the conversation about the slasher from one in which queer audiences see themselves in the work of straight filmmakers to one in which queer artists permutate their cinematic past in new and exciting directions that expand on the slasher's queer history to create a new canon of queer slasher films.

In *Queer Horror Film and Television*, Darren Elliott-Smith raises questions about the history of queer horror scholarship pioneered by authors such as Doty and Benshoff as it applies to emerging queer-produced horror titles with queer characters. While Benshoff uses "the monster queer" to understand how horror films allegorize social anxieties about queer people, Elliott-Smith proposes that horror for queers and by queers shifts this conversation by looking inward to the fears held among contemporary queer communities. He specifically looks at queer men's horror films in terms of disidentification with heteronormative masculinity that disavows femininity and speaks to queer men's fears about being feminine or sexually receptive. To do this, he draws on José Esteban Muñoz's theory of disidentification as a process that complicates binary narratives of identification and counteridentification. Elliott-Smith argues that in these queer horror films "the subject simultaneously recognises himself in the image of an unattainable phallic masculine ideal (simbolised in the heterosexual male) but also acknowledges that it is different from his homosexual self."[10] He looks at the films of David DeCoteau and the gay slasher *Hellbent* (Paul Etheredge, 2004), among others, as examples of queer horror that explores an eroticized heteronormative "straight-acting" masculinity while rendering femininity invisible or still taboo, even among queer films made in the twenty-first century.

In another contemporary study, *Desire after Dark*, Andrew J. Owens makes the case that occult media (including witches and vampires) challenge heteronormative gender and sexuality. Owens begins with a discussion of the sociopolitical shifts of the 1960s sexual revolution in the US intersecting countercultural movements with the ability for occult television such as *Dark Shadows* (1966–71) to critique heteronormative sexuality on screen. He then traces occult media as a decidedly queer expression through to contemporary cable shows with explicitly queer audiences such as the supernatural gay soap opera *Dante's Cove* (2005–07). Owen describes how "these series refract nonnormative sexualities though the conventions of the occult in order to illuminate ambivalent horizons of contemporary queer masculinities and relationships between men."[11] Among these ambivalent depictions is the relatively cliché preservation of masculine gender norms and the continued derision of feminine, receptive sex partners. Owens also expands the question of horror's queer political function given its illicit representations, articulating the possibility for horror to be viewed as problematic within certain frameworks of evaluation seeking positive queer representation, social realism, and orthodoxy. Owens posits instead that "queer orientations toward occult media unearth those pleasures to be found in so-called perversity, abjection, and deviance."[12] I hope to join in this conversation about the precarity of queer horror, particularly the ways in which it seems to at once powerfully reimagine the genre and reaffirm some of its more challenging and regressive logic.

One avenue that helps me think through the nuanced or ambivalent position of a queer horror viewer is that of "perverse" pleasure. Janet Staiger's *Perverse Spectators* theorizes perverse spectatorship as departing from presumed normative reception. She identifies that queer audiences are one such example of this as they tend to invest in extra-diegetic aspects of a film (such as gay men's fascination with Hollywood's leading ladies) and prioritize minor elements of plot that relate to queer experiences.[13] She further explores nonnormative responses to horror informed by personal experience, such as her own experience of laughing "inappropriately" during *The Texas Chainsaw Massacre* (Tobe Hooper, 1974). She observes that "one way to reassure oneself that one is not perverted is to find a community of others—a subculture of like-minded individuals who mirror one's own nature."[14] This perhaps lays the groundwork for thinking about how the extratextual social and cultural experiences of queer individuals lead to the formation of queer horror subcommunities. Audiences whose engagements with horror deviate from normative reception and may be deemed inappropriate by mainstream viewers, such as laughing with Leatherface as he goes about his bloody massacre or feeling tenderly toward him, identifying with him, or turning him into cute fan art.[15]

Whether we love these killers despite their violence or because of it remains ambiguous and perhaps variable among viewers.

Personally, and perhaps surprisingly, I dislike watching scenes of graphic violence. It is not the draw of these films for me nor the reason I identify with their killers. In fact, Murray Smith contends that what he calls truly "perverse allegiance," meaning allegiance with a character strictly because of their illicit actions, is rarer than one may think. He instead outlines strategies that explain the more complex and shifting allegiances viewers are likely to have with characters who transgress morality. Smith speaks of "moral immoralism—the holding up of a particular moral doctrine for ridicule, for the sake of a superior moral claim."[16] He locates this within genre cinema as well as avant-garde queer cinema portraying sex, nudity, and gender nonconforming bodies such as Jack Smith's *Flaming Creatures* (1963), which he calls "an assault on . . . the intolerance of Puritanical moral doctrines and precepts."[17] Smith's characterization of "moral immoralism" helps me to understand a viewership practice more allegiant to the transgression of a specific moral code than to the immoral actions depicted. Additionally, his articulation of this practice within queer cinema offers a way to see the slasher's offense to good taste in line with queer affronts to conservative, heteronormative, and religious moralism. In this book, I argue that the slasher dramatizes a critique of white heteronormative bourgeois suburbs and, in doing so, performs an unlikely queer political function. It may also be said that through its flamboyant violence and reckless sensibilities, the slasher performs the simultaneous function of admonishing moralistic viewers repelled by its garishness. An allegiance to Leatherface or Michael Myers should be seen not only as an allegiance with a killer. It is a complex attachment with an emblem of transgression against a moral system that deems queerness immoral and perverse. Smith notes that his examples of sexually decadent cinema are often uncomfortable as they conjoin representations of queer sexual freedom and bodily autonomy with bleaker images of immorality writ large, such as necrophilia, rape, and nonconsensual sadism.[18] Similarly, the slasher reproduces imagery that is not an intended part of a utopian queer world. Of utmost obviousness among these is its misogynist voyeurism and violence against women. Nonetheless, the slasher offers an uncommon mainstream cinematic form that transgresses the moral systems that villainize queer lives. It depicts immoral acts, but it also antagonizes the very idea of morality.

Queer Slashers is also informed by Judith Butler's arguments about taking a critical stance toward the queer subject and queer language by evaluating their important uses, their unfortunate erasures, and their need to continuously evolve. In "Critically Queer," Butler contends that the term *queer*, as reclaimed among academic and activist communities of the 1990s, must be understood within its historical context and remain open to change, and to the possibility of its future obsolescence. She states, "If the term 'queer' is to be a site of collective contestation, the point of departure for a set of historical reflections and future imaginings, it will have to remain that which is, in the present, never fully owned, but only and always redeployed, twisted, queered from a prior usage and in the direction of urgent and expanding political purposes, and perhaps also yielded in favor of terms that do that political work more effectively."[19] Butler notes here that the term *queer* is not something owned in the present but only a redeployment of *queer* as a historical term of collective stigma with the hope to rework it for different political aims. Butler raises concerns about whether the term *queer* succeeds in regard to its aim to unify marginalized communities. She observes ongoing divides over the term among generations and a failure by the movement to acknowledge its own patriarchal whiteness. Thus, she contends, *queer* potentially fails to be intersectional. She ultimately relates the functional yet fraught complexity of queer to Gayatri Chakravorty Spivak's concept of "the necessary error" of identity, noting that "the political deconstruction of 'queer' ought not to paralyze the use of such terms, but, ideally, to extend its range, to make us consider at what expense and for what purposes the terms are used, and through what relations to power such categories have been wrought."[20] Of particular importance to this book is her recognition that reclamations such as this may be of functional use but are not necessarily ideal nor infinite. Rather, we might discuss how they have been used and what issues may be at stake in these usages. The slasher's place as an imperfect vessel for themes of queer resistance likewise makes such tensions apparent. It may not be the best form to express queer ideologies, but as it has been used in this way, it is certainly worth considering such uses.

Butler further contends that the cultural embrace of queer in the 1990s marked an invocation of stigmatizing language to perform the very critique of that language, a hyperbolic expansion of a homophobic linguistic tradition that hopes to contest homophobia itself. She states, "The subject who is 'queered' into public discourse by homophobic interpellations of various kinds *takes up* or *cites* that very term as the basis for an opposition. This kind of citation will emerge as *theatrical* to the extent that it *mimes and renders hyperbolic* the discursive conventions that is also *reverses.*"[21] She links this with the political hyperbole of "theatrical rage" seen in response to the AIDS crisis and demonstrated through actions such as mass die-ins, which took up and reauthored images of mass queer suffering with ambitions to demonstrate anger about government indifference. She states, "Mobilized by the injuries of homophobia, theatrical rage reiterates those injuries precisely trough an 'acting out,' one that does not merely repeat or recite those injuries, but that deploys a hyperbolic display of death to overwhelm the epistemic resistance to AIDS and to the graphics of suffering."[22] Such theatrical protests flaunted the brutal imagery of queer suffering as a means to state opposition to the deaths they portrayed. Rather than shrinking away from such sights, they amplified them.

In this book, I am looking at slashers as a contextualized cinematic form. One that began as a sign of injury for the queer communities who were commonly positioned by these films as killers but that has since been redeployed by queer filmmakers toward different aims. The term *queer slashers* feels especially apropos as it speaks to the integral connection between the political and academic reclamation of the term *queer* (historically, a term of injury) and queer filmmakers' citation of the slasher (historically, a horror subgenre of injury) when forging ahead in their own creative work. Building from Butler's exploration of the functional yet fraught position of the term *queer*, I will consider how the slasher has been reworked by queer filmmakers in hopes of directing it toward queer political and social aims. I also explore how the slasher is a challenging object that carries long-standing homophobic, transphobic, misogynist, and racist implications. I also respectfully acknowledge that though reclaimed and reworked, queer slashers have not fully severed themselves from these troubling implications and still predominantly reflect a landscape of white gay men. As with Butler, I do not feel this deconstruction needs to halt conversation about these films and their important uses. However, I do hope to keep the category of queer slashers open to necessary discussions of their erasures and their own relationships with discourses of power. While the slasher has been a vessel for queer work, it may not be the ideal vessel. As much as my examination of the form is done with earnest affection, I also question whether this particular vessel serves all marginalized communities aptly and effectively. Perhaps somewhat unexpectedly, my hope is not for more or better queer slashers but for a world where queer slashers become unnecessary as the stigmatizing pain that they respond to no longer forms the basis for so many queer subjectivities. Yet, as I discuss in this book's conclusion, eighteen-year-old trans filmmaker Alice Maio Mackay has recently made *Bad Girl Boogey* (2022), a queer and trans slasher. So, we are evidently still in a place of pain where some queer and trans filmmakers find the slasher to be of use.

I would further like to think of queer slashers in terms of Butler's theory of reclamation as hyperbole, an expansion and proliferation of the homophobic language that forged the queer subject in public discourse. Queer slashers do indeed expand and exaggerate the slasher's homophobia with the aim to contest the very homophobic visual language they expound on. A central mystery about queer people's attachment to the slasher has long been why we would return to a form that positions us as killers, especially why queer filmmakers would see value in representing queers as killers or, conversely, disposable victims of violence. I see the queer slasher as another expression of what Butler calls "theatrical rage." They hyperbolize the homophobia, the government apathy, the social and political abuses that we see in our daily lives and in much of the media depicting queers as long-suffering outsiders and weirdos. Paraphrasing Butler, I see queer slashers as a citation of the slasher form that renders hyperbolic the discursive conventions of the subgenre's homophobic killers and queer victims in order to contest or reverse these paradigms. However, as Butler describes, queer performativity, the intentional reiteration of heterosexual norms as seen in performances such as drag, more accurately reinscribes and perpetuates that which it cites. Such that the drag queen does not end white and cisgender feminine beauty norms but performs them in hyperbolic terms. The struggle is knowing if and when any subversion may occur or if such performances can only reinscribe the norm with an eye toward denaturalizing it through hyperbolic expansion. For Butler, subversion occurs less in the performance itself than in the performance's ability to reshape the concepts of family and community around the acts of performance. She states that "the appropriation and redeployment of the categories of dominant culture enable the formation of kinship relations that function quite supportively as oppositional discourse within that culture."[23] She sees this as "the social and discursive building of community, a community that binds, cares, teaches, shelters, and enables."[24] It is the community, the people within and around the performances, that creates "a more enabling future."[25]

It is for this reason that I want to focus here on the queer film-makers who produce these films and the queer audiences who gather to watch them. While the reworking of the slasher may never fully untether the form from its traumatic past or continued entanglement with troubling discourses of power, the communities of artists and audiences who nurture queer relationships around these objects do substantively transform dominant cultural formations of kinship and family comprising those commonly ostracized from heteronormative nuclear family structures. The supportive communities of horror filmmakers and audiences that develop around these movies create an oppositional discourse through the queer slasher, which may expand on and re-present homophobic pain. Yet what is clearest to me about queer slashers is that those who are drawn to create and watch them find in that endeavor a collective of individuals with compatible traumas and coping strategies. We see other people who were hurt like us and who find in this hyperbolic demonstration of theatrical rage a means to see and understand that trauma better.

Queer Slashers is an account of minoritized queer aesthetics and queer affects produced through and around queer engagements with the slasher film. Methodologically, I use queer theory to give language to the ambiently queer resonances observed in these works that often lack clear verbal explanations. I am not interested in locking in a singular meaning surrounding any of the films in this book. Instead, theory here is meant to offer readers verbiage that may apply to their already existing passions and identifications with the slasher. For example, Butler's theory of queer reclamations of past trauma as "theatrical rage," as discussed in this introduction, gives readers one way to see and understand a potential usefulness for the slasher as a queer style of filmmaking despite its history of queerphobic representations. I see queer theory as a tool to explain what is already happening in practice. The queer audiences for horror, and slashers specifically, are manifest in the myriad queer media produced in their likeness, from documentaries such as *Scream, Queen!* (2019) and *Queer for Fear* (2022), to podcasts such as *Horror Queers* and *Homos on Haunted Hill*, to the recent edited collection of personal essays about horror by queer and trans authors *It Came from the Closet*.[26] This is not an empirical study of queer audiences. For an empirical study of queer horror spectatorship, please see Heather O. Petrocelli's important book *Queer for Fear: Horror Film and the Queer Spectator*, which provides firsthand data from a sample of queer viewers about their tastes and viewing practices.[27] *Queer Slashers* is meant as a tool to better comprehend the queer resonances of the slasher and its many reiterations by queer filmmakers. It cultivates linguistic strategies to articulate what audiences may find queer about the slasher, or how the slasher overlaps with queer themes and queer cultures.

To understand the slasher in terms of queer aesthetics, I will consider it alongside the queer history to which it runs parallel. This means the social and political movements that serve as its historical backdrop as well as the works of queer and countercultural cinema produced in its time. By placing the slasher, a conventionally mainstream and heterosexual horror subgenre, more closely in conversation with the queer culture at the time of its inception and peak popularity, I see an opportunity to better explain how queer artists and audiences come to see themselves in such films. Throughout this book, I engage in what I would call parallel curations of relevant media and history. These are not meant to suggest causation or any form of essential relationship. In fact, in many cases the relationships among these artifacts are created by me alone. I see this act of curation as one methodology to elicit new conceptions of the slasher. In much the way film editing creates meaning by setting one image after the other, enticing the brain to see these spliced frames as having a relation encouraged by the editor's hand, the parallel curations of queer media and historical artifacts throughout this book are meant to spur connections for the reader that may not otherwise come to the fore. Nothing about this book is essential. Nothing is a must. In keeping with the queer spirit of variety and multiplicity in meanings, this book is an invitation to utilize its language and ideas toward heterogenous understandings of its subject.

To understand queer affects around the slasher, I will rely on a more vexing and plainly subjective understanding of these films. I am inspired here by Sianne Ngai's brilliantly clear articulation that "criticism is conceptual justification for feeling based judgments."[28] She credits the idea behind this definition to Stanley Cavell, who states, "Criticism accordingly becomes a work of determining, as it were after the fact, the grounds of (the concepts shaping) pleasure and value in the working of the object."[29] A potential distinction to be made here is the difference between a feeling and an affect. In a key moment of clarification, Brian Massumi describes an affect as "a prepersonal intensity corresponding to the passage from one experiential state of the body to another"[30] Eric Shouse builds on this distinction by delineating affect, in Massumi's terms, from feeling. He notes that "affect precedes will and consciousness," whereas feeling is "personal and biographical," "a sensation that has been checked against previous experiences and labelled."[31] Shouse comments further on the relationship between the two, noting that they are different yet not wholly independent. He credits affect with giving feeling intensity and urgency, stating that "affect is what makes feelings feel."[32] Because affect is "unformed and unstructured (abstract)," he says, it can accumulate power via transmission. By this, he means not the taking on of others' conscious feelings but the ambiently understood underlying bodily resonances among people sharing an unnamed, nonconscious intensity. Perhaps, looking back to Chaskin, something like "osmosis" that allows for collaboration in service of a queer resonance not consciously understood or verbalized. Shouse states that it is affect's "'abstractivity' that makes it transmittable in ways that feelings and emotions are not, and it is because affect is transmittable that it is potentially such a powerful social force."[33] Throughout this book, I try to provide language that helps to narrativize the intense underpinnings of my own queer fascination with the slasher. I rely often on my own experiences to shape this narrative. I invite readers to bring their respective experiences and biographies to this book as well. In the act of narrativizing, one perhaps can provide a conscious cogency to an underlying affective intensity. The work of this book is to piece together larger social, historical, and linguistic strategies that may begin to help one understand the inevitably nebulous and untenable question of the queer meanings of the slasher. Meanings, I argue, that are rooted in the nonverbal and prepersonal intensities of affect.

Queer slashers (the movies) are conceptual justifications for feeling based judgments. They engage through the conscious selection, curation, and redirection of the slasher's queer appeals in acts of critique that transform the slasher from a universalized object in which we may see and experience a queer resonance to a minoritized work of queer critique in which a queer artist offers a version of the slasher that deliberately attunes itself to their own queer experience and the anticipated experiences of a queer audience. The biographies and personal histories of these queer artists and the feelings understood in the context of those histories are instrumental in the re-creation of the slasher into a queer expression. While those narrativized feelings are at work in the conscious choices made here, I nonetheless argue that prepersonal, nonconscious affective intensities of queer engagements with the slasher underlie this conscious practice of refashioning a rusty tool toward a new task. Queer slashers implicitly seek to augment a form that made its appeal known to us in states of being prior to our own queer self-understanding, often in childhood. We knew this was *for* us yet also could not necessarily understand how. And upon more careful and conscious consideration, we confusingly realize that this form is also *against* us. It sees us as killers and monsters. Queer slashers are the material result of a process of self-inquiry about the very nature of this prior affective intensity around the slasher. They imbue the queer self, a personal and verbalized concept of queer identity, into a form that impacts us in a visceral sense that precedes and evades rationalization. In queer slashers, queer audiences see queer artists make a version of this object of shared affective intensity that newly communicates a conscious understanding of the queer position within it. The slasher now comes from the perspective of someone with the lived experience to understand a corresponding queer position in life.

Queer Slashers (the book) is likewise my conceptual justification for feeling based judgments. It is my attempt, through accounts of queer theory, queer history, and queer cinema, to explain from the vantage point of a queer person how these queer-authored forms of the slasher engage with my feelings about the slasher as informed by a queer personal history. It is also, beneath that, an attempt in conscious language to understand as near as possible the impossible underlying intensity that drew me here in the first place. It is a pile of language forged by an adult with a PhD that rests on the earnest curiosities of a lonely queer child. A person who feels belonging in historical slurs used to describe assigned male at birth people who are feminine such as *queen, sissy,* and *faggot.* For whom *queer* is a term about difference as much in gender as in sexuality and whose experience of gender is fraught and traumatic to the point of not knowing what and if that really is anymore. An autistic and ADHD person who has a particularly difficult time staying on topic and not surrendering the page to the white-hot attraction of every emerging new idea as it happens in the moment. To be frank, someone who found it extremely difficult to write this book.

I have decided to embrace a both queer and disordered approach to academic writing throughout this project. To me, a queer approach means trying to unseat monolithic meanings rather than entrench myself within them. This is reflected in my project to open up possibilities for meanings rather than close down conversations to advance a single thread of interpretation. It also takes shape in my interwoven and overlapping treatment of concepts and categorizations such as genre. While many scholars have done the important work of characterizing the US slasher's conventional traits and canonical history, this book is not strongly invested in rigidly defining the slasher or contending with the matter of what is or is not a slasher. This means that at times I welcome the simultaneous explorations of the classical US slasher cycle of 1978–85 as well as the Italian *giallo* and other cinematic styles that incorporate elements of one or both.[34] This is in keeping with the belief that meanings are more completely understood when not limited by binaries. I feel there are important elements of many films brought into clearer focus when they are considered against preexisting categories of study. Characteristics such as voyeuristic first-person camera, masked (or gloved) killers, sequential murders, and sexualized violence (or sexual arousal ending in violence rather than sex) permeate cinema. Considering any film with some or all of these features beside the slasher allows us to understand important things about it. This does not essentialize the film (i.e., argue that it *is* a slasher). However, it helps us see how such traits work complexly throughout films of different kinds and from different countries of origin. The existing category of the slasher is a tool here with which to understand overlapping aspects of films that may otherwise appear disparate.

A disordered approach to writing is newer to me, but it reflects my feeling, learned recently in life, that my earnest inclinations in conveying ideas are not shared by the widest possible audience, and the way things make sense to my brain may appear chaotic to others. As commonly observed, my thinking tends not to move in a linear fashion but instead takes the form of parallel threads that I eventually weave together. These threads look to many readers like tangents or digressions, and perhaps they are. However, in the spirit of queer approaches to academia, I wonder if there are not ideas present in this book, because of my approach, that may not have come into being without my disorders. And I choose to value my neurodivergence as a fruitful part of my process. I also commit here to a queer approach to language. This means to me that there is no one singularly correct method of writing. Important ideas can come from multiple styles of English. In keeping with this, you may notice that I employ unconventional sentence breaks. Fragments, for flair. This is both queer and disordered to me as it queers assumptions about language (and the conventions of grammar that might limit rather than expand creative possibilities) while also embracing the characteristic shortness and exacerbated "to-the-pointness" of being autistic and ADHD. It also errs on the side of universality and accessibility. Academic linguistic conventions can be alienating to some readers. I try my hardest to write for the ear rather than only the eye. I want this book to function as a resource for as wide an audience as possible. I am a reader. I read. And I would be most accommodated by someone who writes as I do, whether this abides academic conventions or not (mostly not).

Having said all that that, I have done my best to organize a thing that will be intelligible to most. It unofficially has two parts. Chapters 1 and 2 attempt to make sense of why the canonical slasher of the 1970s and '80s feels queer. For chapters 3, 4, and 5, each closely examines one queer slasher and seeks to understand how queer slashers work by unpacking the creative choices of this example. These two halves are admittedly written with two rather jarringly different methodologies. The first two chapters take a more conventional and comprehensive approach by casting a wide net and covering a string of related titles over a span of time. They read as composite chapters that give queer historical context and then situate relevant films within this context. Chapters 3 through 5 take one film and engage in vivid close reading of that one film. This is in part because of how I see these two halves differently. The latter half of the book that gives close readings of three respective queer slashers, as in slashers made by queer filmmakers, represents to me the core of the book. It is an exploration of the slasher as a form reiterated by queer artists in new ways that offer commentary and critique. Chapters 1 and 2, for me, are a prelude to these close readings. They provide background that I feel is extremely important to understanding how slashers treat queer themes and may already be seen to serve a queer function even before queers get their hands on them. The second half of the book could also be said to veer closer toward a poetic tone. This is because I take an intimate stance toward the works of these queer artists. Chapters 3 through 5 are intellectual and emotional engagements with the works of queer filmmakers, and each pays tribute to the film and filmmaker through the medium of close reading, as close and loving an eye as my academic training has prepared me to give any work of art. I will engage with the artists themselves as well as their thoughts and feelings about the films. But really, I am writing a love letter to them from one queer to another. And as such, the second half of the book is looser in style and tends to romanticize more often. In order to tether these poetic close readings to a pragmatic pillar, I have seen fit to also draft a conclusion that outlines three wide-reaching trends in queering the slasher, as suggested in chapters 3 through 5. The conclusion allows for clarification about how the film in each of these chapters can be seen as emblematic of what is happening in contemporary queer horror across the board.

Chapter 1, "What Is Queer about the Slasher?" argues the queer lineage and queer function of the canonical slasher cycle of 1978–85. To do this, I articulate a new queer history for the slasher that connects the killers of the 1970s and '80s to their

cinematic predecessors from preslasher films of the 1930s, and
'40s. I consider specifically how these earlier figures establish
tropes of the killer that allow him to be read as queer, especially
by queer audiences. This includes his sexual and gender differences, which draw on psychological discrimination of the period
by conflating queerness with mental illness (and both with murderousness). I also situate the killer POV commonly found in
the slasher within this longer timeline by discussing first-person
camera scenes of murder in these preslasher films, which emphasize patterns of voyeuristic looking in which the killer's gaze
leads to a violent rather than sexual approach. These early homophobic images depicting queer characters as violent deviations
from heterosexuality are further understood within the queer
political context of the 1950s homophile movement, which sought
specifically to remedy these popular misconceptions of queers as
dangerous threats. By identifying these roots for the slasher in the
misrepresentation of queer and gender nonconforming people, I
contend that the history of the slasher's formula is grounded in
queer themes from the outset. Additionally, I argue the slasher
functions queerly by identifying how the subgenre provides a
potent visual manifestation of the post-Stonewall 1970s gay liberation movement to which it was a historical peer. Gay liberation
varied from the homophile movement in its call to oppose (rather
than assimilate into) heteronormative society. This included the
gender role system as well as the oppressive structures of religion, capitalism, and the nuclear family. The slasher, at its core,
stages repetitive collisions of a queer outsider (the killer) and
emblematic figures of heteronormative society. We see this in his
repeated attacks on white middle-class suburban enclaves of the
1980s, his targeting of prom queens and popular jocks as victims,
and his symbolic disenchantment of idyllic adolescent rituals—
prom night, graduation day, and summer camp.

Chapter 2, "What Ever Happened to Christmas?" expands this
queer theory of the slasher by working through its iconoclastic

critique of a ritual rooted in family, religion, and capitalism: Christmas. Building on Eve Kosofsky Sedgwick's important articulation of queerness as a multiplicity of meaning able to be understood in contrast with the monolithic singularity of Christmas, I explore the popular subcategory of Christmas slashers that open up space for different meanings and feelings around the holiday by giddily augmenting its mass-mediated imagery in sexually perverse and violent variations.[35] I draw connections between these slashers and the unique joy of the holiday espoused by queer auteur John Waters in his essay "Why I Love Christmas," which involves encouraging gay queens to go caroling in conservative neighborhoods and replacing the head of the baby Jesus on Christmas cards with that of Charles Manson.[36] Following this thread, I examine the overlap between low-budget slashers of the 1970s and historically parallel queer cinema by Waters, Andy Milligan, and Curtis Harrington. This reveals important stylistic and thematic connections between the slasher and queer cinema of its time, which speaks to the slasher's queer appeal. While Leatherface's cross-dressing Ed Gein aesthetic terrorized audiences in Tobe Hooper's 1974 film *The Texas Chainsaw Massacre*, so too did murderous drag queen Divine that same year in Waters's *Female Trouble*. Looking more closely at these parallels, I develop a theory of the queer countercultural aspects of murder and filth in this post-Stonewall moment. By considering Sedgwick's theory of queer as being about "loose ends" rather than "lining up," I explain the distinct queerness in resisting normative definitions of taste, just as we are rethinking sexuality.[37] These threads come together in a discussion of the widely overlooked Christmas slasher *Silent Night, Bloody Night* (1972), which embodies this queer critique of Christmas while also emerging from an unexpected queer production context. Its director, Theodore Gershuny, cast his then wife, Warhol Factory star Mary Waronov, in the lead role and notably utilized other queer artists and Factory stars, such as Ondine, Jack Smith, and

Tally Brown, in cameo roles as exploited hospital patients who rebel against their oppressors.

In chapter 3, "The Sun Will Come Out Tomorrow, or Will It?" I argue that John Waters's 1994 film *Serial Mom* playfully subverts the slasher's characterization of queer people as killers. In *No Future*, Lee Edelman theorizes a queer antisocial position rooted in his observation that queers are differentiated from heterosexuality by their nonreproductive sex and therefore are commonly burdened with the cultural death drive. The Child, he argues, represents an ideal of reproduction and futurity while the queer is burdened with an expectation of finitude.[38] The slasher formula wherein a queer outsider terrorizes and kills the children of white middle-class families seems an apt visual expression of Edelman's argument. Yet Waters's revision turns this on its head, transforming hypernormative suburban mom Beverly Sutphin (Kathleen Turner) into the film's killer. While queers have long been the killers of the slasher, Waters recasts the role with a figure who, from a queer perspective, poses a true threat: a cis straight white suburban mom who perpetuates the oppressive normativity of capitalism and the nuclear family. I consider Beverly beside wholesome TV commercial mom and antiqueer activist Anita Bryant, whose 1970s public platform proliferated dangerous messages linking queer people to child sexual abuse. Comparatively, sexual deviants, punks, and horror gore-hounds are harmless and fun in *Serial Mom*. White suburban middle-class culture is the killer. I further offer José Esteban Muñoz's *Cruising Utopia* as a counterpoint to Edelman's structure that encourages us to step out of straight time and imagine a tangible utopian queer future.[39] In a reading of Waters's film, particularly of its scene of murder set to the ambivalently hopeful "Tomorrow" from the musical *Annie*, I observe that the queer slasher steps out of straight time to imagine what the slasher could be. That it takes a historically queerphobic cinematic form and instead seeks to envision a slasher that serves queer audiences by naming the right killer.

Chapter 4, "What the Fuck Is Wrong with You?" looks at the conflicted position of the queer spectator of the slasher as someone with a personal attachment to films that commonly display traits of misogyny and homophobia. Specifically, I look at Peaches Christ (Joshua Grannell), a drag performer who produces stage parodies of cult horror films and the director of the queer slasher *All About Evil* (2010). In the film, Peaches plays a version of herself, a San Francisco horror movie maven and hostess. When confronting one of the film's killers who is also dressed in drag, Peaches remarks with disgust, "What the fuck is wrong with you?" *All About Evil* dramatizes the distinct difference between horror drag (the camp performance of horror in theatrical contexts) and the cinematic legacy of the queer killer (a violent and dangerous history that villainizes queer people and associates their sexualities with murderous tendencies). I look at the film in the context of Richard Dyer's category of pastiche, a form that amplifies both likeness and discrepancy from its source material by reiterating the style of its referent while also making meaningful departures that call attention to the pastiche author's perspective.[40] Merging Dyer's pastiche with Judith Butler's theory of drag as a reiteration of heteronormativity that seeks to achieve mastery within it, I argue *All About Evil* performs a cinematic act of drag by reiterating the slasher's harmful queer stereotypes while also amplifying the clear differences between the canonical slasher and subsequent queer slashers.[41] Christ conceptualizes drag as the celebration of both the queer performer and the person they honor, be it a horror icon like Freddy Krueger or a grand diva like Judy Garland. Through her work, she theorizes a style of queer horror performance that distinguishes itself from degrading representations of queer killers by celebrating the self-described "weird queer" underneath, who uses horror imagery to profess their positive feelings of difference and collective unity with a nonnormative community.

In chapter 5, "Why Do We Go into the Woods?" I look at the sincere and complex exploration of dangerous queer sexuality in *Stranger by the Lake* (Alain Guiraudie, 2013). Interestingly, this exploration of the slasher from a queer perspective varies the pattern of characterizing the killer as a queer outsider. Instead, the film has a razor-sharp focus on the queer subcommunity of a gay cruising beach, with both killer and victims being parts of the same sexual ecosystem. Whereas scholarship on the canonical slasher emphasizes the way that the killer's violent approach can be seen as an impotent imitation of heterosexuality where the sexual impulse is subsumed into the violent act (as in Leatherface revving his chainsaw that just won't start), *Stranger by the Lake* queers this construction by instead subsuming the violent impulse into its sexuality.[42] Sex is mundane and everywhere in this queer space. What is coveted and dangerously taboo is instead the self-destructive lure of violence. As such, *Stranger by the Lake* creates a uniquely queer slasher, not by refusing the implications of a queer history with dangerous sexuality but by considering this history in an intimate and emotionally vivid way. Drawing on gay histories of cruising and the especially dangerous period of sexuality amid the AIDS crisis, this queer slasher asks queer men an important question: "Why do we go into the woods?" (i.e., why do we seek or allow dangerous encounters?). I discuss the cruising beach as an example of a queer counterpublic that allows for new models of sociality in which sex is a part of public life.[43] The allure of the killer then signifies a contrasting pull away from this new queer society and toward a self-immolating powerlessness that can be understood through Leo Bersani's work on sacrificing the internalized phallic male ego.[44] Finally, I consider *Stranger by the Lake* as an example of "negative" media with a backward-looking logic best explained by Heather Love's *Feeling Backward*.[45] I propose that these negative representations are part of a healthy relationship with the homophobia of the present and past that does not disavow this trauma but rather chooses to reexperience it. This decision is itself mirrored in the artist's and audience's choice not to select a warm or happy cinematic form of expression but instead to repeatedly recommit to the pain and violence found in the slasher.

NOTES

1. See Harry Benshoff's chapter "Satan Spawn and Out and Proud" in *Monsters in the Closet: Homosexuality and the Horror Film* (Manchester: Manchester University Press, 1997).

2. To his credit, costar Robert Englund openly discusses in the documentary that he fully understood he was playing the film as homoerotic, explaining his choices to caress Patton's beautiful face and his request to insert the blade of Krueger's glove in Patton's mouth to simulate fellatio.

3. Eric N, "David Chaskin," *Bloody Good Horror*, September 19, 2007, http://www.bloodygoodhorror.com/bgh/interviews/09/19/2007/david-chaskin.

4. Eric N, "David Chaskin."

5. Eric N, "David Chaskin."

6. Eve Kosofsky Sedgwick, *Epistemology of the Closet* (Berkeley: University of California Press, 1990), 1, 20–21.

7. Alexander Doty, *Making Things Perfectly Queer: Interpreting Mass Culture* (Minneapolis: University of Minnesota Press, 1993), 15.

8. Benshoff, *Monsters in the Closet*, 6.

9. Benshoff, 12–13.

10. Darren Elliott-Smith, *Queer Film and Television: Sexuality and Masculinity at the Margins* (London: I. B. Tauris, 2016), 7.

11. Andrew J. Owens, *Desire after Dark: Contemporary Queer Cultures and Occultly Marvelous Media* (Bloomington: Indiana University Press, 2021), 183.

12. Owens, *Desire after Dark*, 6.

13. Janet Staiger, *Perverse Spectators: The Practices of Film Reception* (New York: New York University Press, 2000), 37.

14. Staiger, *Perverse Spectators*, 181.

15. The depth of fan art transforming cinematic killers of the slasher into cute versions of themselves is remarkable and deserves its own extensive study. However, as a start, consider the work of Travis Falligrant (@ibtrav), whose multimedia art series *Horror Babies* imagines killers such as Freddy and Jason as adorable toddlers, and Janie Lee (@junkmixart), whose web comic *Camp Counselor Jason* depicts a knife-wielding Jason

who becomes a helpful camp counselor to make sure no children ever drown again at Camp Crystal Lake.

16. Murray Smith, "Gangsters, Cannibals, Aesthetes, or Apparently Perverse Allegiances," in *Passionate Views: Film, Cognition, and Emotion*, eds. Carl Plantinga and Greg M. Smith (Baltimore, MD: Johns Hopkins University Press, 1999), 230.

17. Smith, "Gangsters, Cannibals," 231.

18. Smith, 231.

19. Judith Butler, "Critically Queer," *GLQ* 1, no. 1 (1993): 19.

20. Butler, "Critically Queer," 20.

21. Butler, 23.

22. Butler, 23–24.

23. Butler, 28.

24. Butler, 28.

25. Butler, 29.

26. Joe Vallese, ed., *It Came from the Closet: Queer Reflections on Horror*, (New York: Feminist Press at the City University of New York, 2022).

27. Heather O. Petrocelli, *Queer for Fear: Horror Film and the Queer Spectator* (Cardiff: University of Wales Press, 2023).

28. Sianne Ngai, *Theory of the Gimmick: Aesthetic Judgment and Capitalist Form* (Cambridge, MA: Harvard University Press, 2020), 331.

29. Stanley Cavell, *Philosophy the Day after Tomorrow* (Cambridge, MA: Harvard University Press, 2005), 67.

30. Brian Massumi, "Notes on the Translation and Acknowledgements," in Gilles Deleuze and Felix Guattari, *A Thousand Plateaus: Capitalism and Schizophrenia* (Minneapolis: University of Minnesota Press, 1987), xvi.

31. Eric Shouse, "Feeling, Emotion, Affect," *M/C Journal* 8, no. 6 (2005).

32. Shouse, "Feeling, Emotion, Affect."

33. Shouse.

34. For a discussion of the stylistic overlap between Italian giallo and US slasher films, see Adam Lowenstein, "The Giallo/Slasher Landscape: *Ecologia Del Delitto*, *Friday the 13th* and Subtractive Spectatorship," in *Italian Horror Cinema*, eds. Stefano Baschiera and Russ Hunter (Cardiff, Wales: Edinburgh University Press, 2016), 127–44.

35. Eve Kosofsky Sedgwick, *Tendencies* (Durham, NC: Duke University Press, 1993), 5.

36. John Waters, *Crackpot: The Obsessions of John Waters* (New York: Macmillan, 1986), 116–20; and Melissa Locker, "A Christmas Conversation

with John Waters," *TIME*, December 10, 2013, http://entertainment.time
.com/2013/12/10/a-christmas-conversation-with-john-waters.

37. Sedgwick, *Tendencies*, 8.

38. Lee Edelman, *No Future: Queer Theory and the Death Drive* (Durham, NC: Duke University Press, 2004), 4.

39. José Esteban Muñoz, *Cruising Utopia: The Then and There of Queer Futurity* (New York: NYU Press, 2009), 26.

40. Richard Dyer, *Pastiche* (New York: Routledge, 2007), 55–58.

41. Judith Butler, *Bodies That Matter: On the Discursive Limits of Sex* (New York: Routledge, 1993), 128–37.

42. Robin Wood, *Hollywood from Vietnam to Reagan* (New York: Columbia University Press, 1986), 91; and Carol J. Clover, *Men, Women, and Chain Saws: Gender in the Modern Horror Film* (Princeton, NJ: Princeton University Press, 1992), 186.

43. As described in Lauren Berlant and Michael Warner, "Sex in Public," *Critical Inquiry* 24, no. 2 (winter 1998), 547–66.

44. Leo Bersani, "Is the Rectum a Grave?" *October* 43 (winter 1987), 197–222.

45. Heather Love, *Feeling Backward: Loss and the Politics of Queer History* (Cambridge, MA: Harvard University Press, 2007).

WHAT IS QUEER ABOUT THE SLASHER?

THE SLASHER HAS HISTORICALLY BEEN understood as a subgenre of the horror film that peaked in popularity between 1978 and 1986, beginning with the release of John Carpenter's *Halloween* and continuing through a spate of popular imitators and sequels.[1] Conventions for the subgenre vary by account, but the consensus suggests that these films revolve around a masked killer stalking and murdering a group of teenagers in a suburban middle-class community. Often the killer has suffered a past trauma at the hands of this community and is returning for vengeance. The killer's past is typically shown in an opening flashback scene before transitioning to his present-day sequence of murders. Killers are mostly men, though they are sometimes women or visually gender nonconforming without a verbalized gender identity. The survivor or survivors of the killer are typically the most competent of the group of teenagers, often differentiated through their intelligence or deviation from the attitudes and behaviors of their peers.[2] A prominent thread in popular discussions of the slasher argues that teenagers, especially women, are punished for sex in these films. Therefore, only virgins survive. In scholarship, this popular discourse takes shape in Robin Wood's discussion of the slasher movie as reactionary "teenie kill pic" and Carol J. Clover's theorization of the survivor as "final girl," a uniquely "boyish" girl who is differentiated by her masculine traits and lack of sexual activity.[3]

There has always been tension around the slasher film's difficult subject matter and seemingly reactionary traits. Among them the systematic murder of women, often in scenes with connotations of sexual violence, as well as the villainization of queer characters through their gender nonconforming killers. Yet despite the temptation to abandon the subgenre for its problematic material, queer scholars have continued to discuss the slasher as a relevant popular subgenre.[4] Simply put, many queer and trans people like slasher movies, and many do not. In considering the complexities of the slasher, I would like to speak here with respect for my friends, colleagues, and inspirations who have felt their way through horror's unusually queer resonances. To me, resonance characterizes the subjectively felt ambiently queer energy of films that draw us to them even though logically they might more easily push us away. Go sometime to a Peaches Christ stage show and see a drag queen lip sync "Sweet Dreams (Are Made of This)" dressed as Freddy Krueger. More recently, try to unpack the complex internet meme-ability of the gay Babadook and gay Pennywise. This queer appeal has an objectively verifiable presence, and as such we must assess it with sincerity and dignity. I hope this research will please my queer peers in horror most of all.

In this chapter, I argue that two important features help shape a cohesive understanding of the perceived queerness of the slasher subgenre. The first is its queer lineage, which draws connections between the classical slasher cycle of the 1970s and '80s and earlier, stylistically similar thrillers with queer traits. The second is a theorization of the slasher's queer function. This latter section argues that the slasher formula cyclically stages a confrontation between a social outsider, commonly gender nonconforming and/or sexually nonnormative, and a heteronormative white middle-class suburban enclave, thereby dramatizing in repetitive patterns a queer approach to dismantling conservative norms.

Throughout this book, I use *queer* as an inclusive term for all LGBTQIA+ identities. I also use *queer* as a term that builds on an intersectional and antinormative queer politics as set forth by scholars such as Michael Warner and Cathy Cohen.[5] By this definition, queerness is not opposite to straightness but rather opposite to normativity. A queer politics therefore must operate in service of the liberation of all marginalized identities. In my discussions of how the slasher functions queerly by staging collisions between a queer outsider (the killer) and normative communities (his victims), I speak of a critique of normativity found in these films that is not limited in its usefulness only to LGBTQIA+ communities. The target of such a critique includes heteronormative positions about gender and sexuality but also patriarchal white bourgeois politics that affect a wider array of marginalized communities. Importantly, *queer* here includes all LGBTQIA+ identities but meaningfully recognizes the organic intersections between LGBTQIA+ communities and marginalized communities identified by gender, race, class, and disability. I also want to transparently recognize that the slasher does not do its work equally for all of these intersectional communities. By this I mean that it in many ways preserves concepts of misogyny, racism, and ableism and is therefore not an ideal tool for dismantling structures of power. However, the critique I outline in this chapter may speak in some ways to multiple overlapping communities (though not all, and not equally).

PART ONE: QUEER LINEAGE

The popularly acknowledged precursors to the slasher cycle of 1978–86 come from immediately preceding films with obvious narrative, stylistic, and thematic similarities such as *Black Christmas* (Bob Clark, 1974), *The Texas Chainsaw Massacre* (Tobe

Hooper, 1974), and *The Town That Dreaded Sundown* (Charles B. Pierce, 1976). These films and others feature a killer, typically masked, pursuing adolescent targets: sorority sisters, small-town high schoolers, etc. They provide evidence that the trends associated with the slasher had cinematic expression before its wave of popularity hit and, in fact, were perhaps already brewing when *Halloween* arrived. Rather than seeing *Halloween* as a foundation to which we might compare all '70s and '80s slashers, it is more reasonable to identify the John Carpenter film as an emblematic indicator of a building phenomenon based on earlier trends. In his historical account of the slasher, Richard Nowell notes particularly that many of the seemingly instantaneous *Halloween* imitators such as *When a Stranger Calls* (Fred Walton, 1979) and *The Silent Scream* (Denny Harris, 1979) either were in production or had already completed filming at the time *Halloween* became a major success.[6] This affirms that while *Halloween* was crucial in escalating the popularity of the slasher and likely did lead to an increase in subsequent films of this type, it was not alone in formulating the key traits of the subgenre.

Studies that identify earlier cinematic influences on the slasher commonly focus on Alfred Hitchcock's *Psycho* (1960), which has often been cited as a transformative moment in horror.[7] *Psycho*'s influence is undeniable as it spawned a horde of films attempting to tap into its brand of psychological horror, including some that overtly paraphrased its plot and themes, such as William Castle's *Homicidal* (1961), shot and distributed within a year of *Psycho*'s release. Yet *Psycho* did not come from nowhere. Several critics have traced a broader history for the themes that *Psycho* catapulted to prominence within the horror lexicon. This includes William Schoell's category of "shocker" films that traces *Psycho*'s shocking shower scene back to classical Hollywood and John McCarty's "psycho-film" that makes a case for an overarching pattern of "psycho" characters in horror.[8] While these larger timelines are important in helping us understand the history to which *Psycho* and *Halloween* belong, precursor studies have not yet substantially engaged with the strong case the extension of the slasher timeline makes for recognizing the subgenre's history of queer resonances.

The killer in the canonical slasher cycle has often been categorized as in some way gender nonconforming or sexually non-normative.[9] This is perhaps most evident in the layers of gender performance depicted in killers, which range from conventionally feminine attire worn by killers perceived as men to presenting as a different gender than that assigned at birth. This includes the wigs and makeup donned by Leatherface (Gunnar Hansen) in *The Texas Chainsaw Massacre* (1974), the revelation that Kenny (Derek McKinnon) in *Terror Train* (Roger Spottiswoode, 1980) has appeared throughout the film dressed as a woman, or that Angela (Felissa Rose) in *Sleepaway Camp* (Robert Hiltzik, 1983) is a person who was assigned male at birth but was raised as a girl. A particularly sensitive problem with each of these films is that they are often unspecific and uncaring toward the nuances of gender identity at stake in such representations. They are also obviously subject to the more limited conventions for describing gender nonconforming and trans expressions at the time of their production, compared with queer language developed to address the current spectrum of gender identity and gender expression. This creates an unfortunate difficulty in discussing these characters with respect for the specifics of how they identify. And so, often we are left able to talk only about how they present in terms of gender. Meaning, for example, we understand that Angela presents as male at the start of the film (when we see them as a young boy) but later presents as female (when we meet them at camp).[10] We cannot conclusively discern a gender identity for this character or others like them. It is impossible to distinguish when a character would be accurately described as cross-dressing or whether they are exhibiting a trans identity. And so, speaking collectively, I aim to reflect on the ways in which all of these gender nonconforming behaviors—that is, those that resist or renegotiate assigned binary gender identity—consistently inflect the killer with aspects of queerness.

Even for those killers with less overtly gender nonconforming traits, there remains a precedent for describing the nature of the killer in terms that emphasize dissonance with gender norms. Carol J. Clover argues the killer and the ultimate survivor, or final girl, are inverses. Where she is "boyish" and becomes increasingly phallicized throughout the film as she takes up weapons to fight, he is feminized and loses his phallus, becoming symbolically castrated at the end of the film.[11] Jack Halberstam observes, from a less heteronormative perspective on power, that what the survivors and the killer have in common is their mutual queerness. Rather than seeing the surviving character as "boyish," Halberstam contends they have been "de-girled" and assimilated into a postgender and even posthuman landscape. It is "properly gendered" bodies (i.e., heteronormative bodies) that are doomed to die in the slasher while those that resist norms persevere. While a killer like Michael Myers is not known for a hyperfeminine aesthetic—though the clown-white mask and powder puff wig do provide just a touch of drag—he belongs to this same pattern of representation that posits queerness as contingent to survival.

We also see in films such as *The Burning* (Tony Maylam, 1981) and *A Nightmare on Elm Street* (Wes Craven, 1984) killers who are associated with both working-class employment and physical disability. *Elm Street*'s janitor turned killer Freddy Krueger and *Burning*'s vengeful camp counselor Cropsy are both scarred from fires set by members of the heteronormative communities they return to attack. While queerness in this book is most centrally referring to non-normative gender and sexuality, we must also respect the roles of class, race, and disability in framing otherness within this context. As Angela Smith very importantly reminds us, discussions of metaphorical otherness in the horror film draw

on a eugenic logic that presumes disability and physical difference to be innately equated with otherness. Therefore, any queer
subtext relies on the enmeshed connections between marginalized positions such as queer and disabled.[12]

Not all killers manifest queer traits in the same ways, nor are
there any universal constants across all slashers. However, the
slasher does seem to consistently evoke queer aspects of nonnormative gender and sexuality through its representations of
killers and their survivors. Quite a lot of these tendencies make
logical sense when we consider how Hitchcock's *Psycho* (1960),
which is seen as a shared forebear to this cinematic movement,
popularized the conceit of a gender nonconforming killer. In
the film, Norman Bates (Anthony Perkins) dresses as his dead
mother and murders Marion Crane (Janet Leigh) in the shower.
As a character, Bates evokes rhetoric about gay men as mother-
obsessed or ruined by domineering mothers.[13] He also draws
heavily on an emerging cultural fascination with trans identity,
fueled in the 1950s by news coverage of serial killer Ed Gein, who
was speculated to "want to be a woman," and trans pioneer Christine Jorgensen, whose transition made national news. Bates particularly borrows from the Gein mythos, as magazines claimed
that Gein wore women's skin to feel like a woman. Though research has shown there appears to be no certain factual basis for
this aspect of Gein's crimes, it was widely repeated at the time.[14] A
1957 *LIFE* pictorial showcasing Gein's "house of horrors" stated,
"He often wished, he said, that he were a woman. Psychiatrists
studying his actions believe he is schizophrenic, or split personality."[15] These consecutive sentences reflect the historical medi-
calization of trans identity as mental illness and further conflate
both transness and mental illness with murderousness.[16] Bates's
expression dressed as his mother is notably tied to his murderous
tendencies, with the mother persona serving as the killer of the
film, not Norman. Jorgensen offered a sincerer trans identity for
the public eye when her return from Denmark was met with the

New York Daily News headline "Ex-GI Becomes Blonde Beauty" in December 1952. Jorgensen's conventional beauty and winning personality made her a celebrity, including appearances on TV talk shows and a successful nightclub act.[17] Her notoriety was briefly reenergized in 1959, shortly before the release of *Psycho*, when she was denied a marriage license because she could not prove her legal sex as female.[18]

The idea of a potentially trans or cross-dressing gender non-conforming killer has been repeated by many of *Psycho*'s imitators. *Homicidal* features a notable turn by actress Joan Marshall, under the pseudonym Jean Arless, playing a dual role as both a man and a woman. The film's killer, Emily/Warren, is represented as two different people, both played by Arless, until the climax of the film—which, like *Psycho*, reveals Emily and Warren not only as the killer but as the same person. We learn in a peculiar account by Lt. Miller (Gilbert Green) that Emily/Warren was born female, but their sex was entered as male as part of a plot by their mother to allow Emily/Warren to inherit their wealthy father's fortune. If Emily/Warren were legally identified as female, then the inheritance would instead pass to Miriam, Emily/Warren's older half sister. Warren is said to have created the Emily persona as a scapegoat on which to blame all the film's murders. In passing, Lt. Miller remarks that Emily emerged following Warren's return after time spent in Denmark, and "what happened there, we don't know." What is especially strange about the ending of *Homicidal* is that it is built around an impossibility. We see Emily/Warren shot, seemingly fatally, as we never learn of their survival. Then, in an echo of the closing scene of *Psycho*, where Dr. Richman (Simon Oakland) explains the events of the film via the confession of Norman's mother persona, Lt. Miller gives the details of Emily/Warren's deception and murder spree—which, the lieutenant says, was designed to kill everyone who knew the truth about Emily/Warren and successfully did so. This begs the obvious question: If everyone who knows this story is dead, how can it

Fig 1.1 An unsubtle news headline seeking a killer who looks an awful lot like Emily in *Homicidal* (1961). Visible in the bottom right corner is the figure of a wedding-topper bridegroom Emily has decapitated during a moment of rage.

be told to us now? One possible way to understand this scenario is that to a heteronormative onlooker, a body of what appears to be a man, Warren, with a vagina might be rationalized through legal means that dismiss gender nonconformity and trans identity. The film seems deeply aware of an appeal that it is making to transness through its light adaptation of *Psycho*'s Gein-like narrative and with its carefully planted reference to Emily emerging after a trip to Denmark, where Jorgensen famously had her gender-affirming surgeries. The film leaves open an opportunity to fill this plot gap with queer knowledge by interpreting the enigma of Emily/Warren to truly be one in which gender expression and gender identity resist heteronormative conventions. This includes the potential that Emily/Warren was a trans woman or a trans man, trans nonbinary, or intersex.[19]

While we can locate the legacy of *Psycho* in many of the queer and gender nonconforming killers that followed, there is a rich history of these character types prior to Hitchcock's pivotal film.

Reconnecting these earlier characters with their more famous progeny brings to the fore new textures in this deeper history of conflating killer/queer inclinations. Among the pioneers of killer/queer characters is Hitchcock's own UK film *The Lodger* (1927), based loosely on Jack the Ripper, the late nineteenth-century killer known for sadistically murdering and then dismembering sex workers in London. The Ripper provides an early example of deviant sexuality in killer tales, linking departures from sexual norms with murderous inclinations. *The Lodger* focuses on a serial killer murdering blonde showgirls. A mysterious lodger, played by queer actor Ivor Novello, is strongly suspected of being the killer. In the adapted Marie Belloc Lowndes novel and early versions of the film, the lodger was guilty.[20] However, in the final film, he is persecuted as a suspect only to be exonerated later. Novello's soft features and pale beauty, like a matinee idol Nosferatu, evoke a queer presence on screen—a fact that is punctuated by the Buntings, who house the lodger, remarking, "He may be a bit queer, but he's a gentleman." Oddness and femininity are the tokens by which the lodger becomes a suspect.

Some key traits of *The Lodger* reoccur in many similar thrillers of this period. The first is a dramatization of sexualized violence against women, which is also then used to indicate non-normative sexuality. Another is the use of a queer actor to signal difference through his softness, his "strangeness." Third is the fascination with knowing and uncovering the secret of the killer, a process that lends itself to queer meaning by echoing the condition of "the closet." In most of these films, the killer's violence is not detected at first. He is seen as respectable, if a bit odd (a doctor, professor, etc.), and only through inspection does his killer/queer identity emerge. He hides his sexual difference along with his murderousness, and they are typically portrayed as inextricably linked.

In the 1943 Jacques Tourneur feature *The Leopard Man*, the killer dons claws to pass off his murders as the acts of an escaped leopard. This killer, we eventually learn, is Dr. Galbraith (James Bell), a mysterious man noted in the film for his soft and fey characteristics. Upon meeting him, we learn he was a college professor, but he'd had to leave his occupation due to unexplained circumstances that suggest impropriety. In a well-positioned turn of phrase, when asked by theater actress Kiki (Jean Brooks) about his departure from college, he returns evasively, "I don't see why you should be interested in my rotten, dusty career . . . when you lead such a gay and exciting life." Then, he gleefully emits a tale of how he once waited outside the theater just to see Mrs. Leslie Carter come out after her performance in *Zaza*. Galbraith's portrayal as an effete theater-loving intellectual positions him clearly as a nonheteronormative figure in the film. As a zoologist and former professor, Galbraith becomes a key resource in the investigation of his own murders, prompting him to reflect on the kind of man who would do these things. When asked by the film's main character, affable would-be detective Jerry (Dennis O'Keefe), if there was a history of men with "kinks in their brains," Galbraith confirms the lineage of killers of which he is a part. He states, "Yes, there have been men who killed for pleasure, strange pleasure. There was Bluebeard in France, Jack the Ripper in London. It's not uncommon." This dialogue interestingly connects violence to sexuality, highlighting the phrase "strange pleasure," which suggests a perverse sexuality tied to a murderous desire. Galbraith is both killer and queer. His urge to murder is tied to his sexuality. This "strange pleasure" tends to take the form of an aroused sexual interest in women that is somehow negated, or perverted, from the more conventional outcome of heterosexual sex and instead satisfied through physical violence.

The relation between the killer and voyeuristic looking in these preslasher films connects them to two important conventions of the canonical '70s and '80s slasher cycle: the stylistic use of first-person POV camera to position the audience in the place of the killer and the linkage between voyeuristic looking and sexualized violence. One prominent example is John Brahm's 1944 remake of Hitchcock's *The Lodger* starring queer actor Laird Cregar as the titular character, Mr. Slade, who this time *is* the killer. Another is Robert Siodmak's *The Spiral Staircase*, released in 1946, starring George Brent as a killer who murders women and people with disabilities as a means of purging the weakness his father taught him to hate in himself and others. In both films, the identity of the killer is withheld until the end of the film, as with *The Leopard Man*. The queerness of the killers is developed throughout the films and then ultimately linked to their murderousness. In *The Spiral Staircase*, two brothers, Albert (Brent) and Steven (Gordon Oliver), discuss the legacy of their father, who taught them to value hypermasculinity and loathe femininity. Steven states, "You know, I'm inclined to think that father was disappointed by both of us. Neither of us fitted his concept of what a real man should be: a gun toting, hard drinking, tough living, God fearing citizen. He always used to say, 'The strong survive, the weak die.'" Of the two, Albert is the one presented as effeminate. He is yet another professor and demonstrates much less interest in courting women than his brother. When Albert reveals he is the killer, he makes clear what he is doing, explaining that his father would be proud to see him destroying the weakness in the world, weakness he associates with femininity and disability. Both are found in his final intended victim: Helen, a woman who cannot speak. As with Albert, Cregar's killer in *The Lodger* is never really a suspect due to his perceived respectability. Cregar performs a sad and perverse queer attachment to Slade's deceased brother, whose demise he blames on the scheming manipulations of evil women. Fetching a portrait of his brother, Slade offers, "I can show you something more beautiful than a beautiful woman. . . . I had a brother, and he was a genius, and I loved him very dearly" before rhapsodizing about the dead man's face and brow and then turning slightly dark, remarking, "He had strange eyes. . . . He was a strange man."[21] The heated and incestuous connotations of Slade's affection become linked to his desire to kill as he describes to the Bontings' daughter Kitty (Merle Oberon), a showgirl, that she has the kind of beauty that could ruin men (as he claimed happened to his brother) and that he wants to cut out the evilness from her, leaving only the beauty behind. The film's climactic scene shows Kitty dancing in her cabaret act to "Parisian Trot" while Slade watches her with an aroused, frenzied desperation. The scene cuts between shots of Kitty dancing and Slade watching her, with each shot of Slade pushing in closer on his face, suggesting a mounting intensity in his gaze. It is in this moment of attraction that Slade determines he must kill Kitty, though he is ultimately unsuccessful.

Slade's arousal, though connotatively sexual, is instead rooted in disgust for his own femininity, his weakness (as Albert calls it). He projects this disgust onto the bodies of women and makes a violent approach that mirrors a predatory sexual advance. One that ultimately disrupts the path toward a sexual assault and instead deploys a phallic knife.[22] Carol J. Clover argues the weapon in the slasher often possesses a phallic undertone and that it operates not with but apart from sexual assault, noting that "slasher killers are by generic definition sexually inadequate—men who kill precisely because they cannot fuck."[23] In the moments of Slade watching Kitty dance, with rapidly increasing intensity, I observe an expression of this inverse sexual interest defined by a sexual fecklessness or effeminacy. It seems totally perverse here that all parties involved—women and queers—appear mistreated by these patterns. Women are made systematic victims of violence, and queer men, or gender nonconforming feminine people, are written as dysfunctional and violent caricatures. Yet the poignancy of a queer actor, such as Cregar, in a role that resonates with queer meaning carries an appeal that I and others still succumb to and wish to explore further.

Importantly, the pattern of first looking and then attacking is a definitive trait of the slasher, seen in Michael Myers's stalking of Laurie Strode (Jamie Lee Curtis) in *Halloween* and, of course, Norman Bates's spying through a peephole as Marion showers before killing her as his mother. In Dr. Richman's expositional monologue, he explains mother was jealous and meant to destroy anyone who sexually aroused her son in order to keep him for herself, a possessive if not altogether incestuous motive. Arousal is not the only motivation conveyed by looking, though. *The Spiral Staircase* contains one of the most intimate killer/viewer associations of any of these films, and it suggests a motive to kill that seems more about self-identification with the culturally loathed weakness of the woman, not any displaced sexual desire. Throughout the movie, the camera commonly pushes in on a shot of the killer's leering eye and then superimposes images of what the eye sees over its iris. In a unique occurrence, we see not just Helen being watched from the POV of the killer inside the eye's iris but, additionally, his imagining of Helen as a face without a mouth. We are shown not only his physical perspective but his psychological perspective as well, emphasizing his obsession with her disability. As we learn later, he sees in Helen a reflection of his own weakness, and in that sense his obsessive imagining of her may appear sexual at first but can also be a sign of his own self-imagining as weak, as woman. I am also thinking here about queer boys' imaginative fascinations with women, the obsessiveness of which may be misread by heteronormative logic as sexual attraction. As any of us who hung posters of Britney Spears on our bedroom walls might know, we looked at her a little differently than our mothers thought. In truth, when the killer looks here and sees Helen without a mouth, he sees her weakness but really his weakness. He sees her as himself.

While the use of POV is complicated and certainly does not offer a 1:1 ratio of seeing as the killer therefore being the killer, it is a distinct departure from the norms of traditional continuity editing. Classical Hollywood editing emphasized patterns of establishing shots and alternating shot/reverse shot structures. Its

Fig 1.2 A psychological close-up on Helen in *The Spiral Staircase* (1946) superimposed over the killer's eye to show how he sees her: without a mouth.

common goal was a neutral, invisible aesthetic that minimized the camera's presence in the frame. A smash cut to a shaking camera that mirrors the gait of a walking person (with the limited visual scope of their line of vision) feels incredibly odd and stands out to us as viewers because it announces the presence of the camera so forcefully. If nothing else, it signals a particular interest in calling our attention to the way the killer sees. Even putting us in the killer's perspective during scenes of murder. We see a scene like this in *The Lodger* (1944), for example, wherein the camera moves in a jerky motion, mimicking human steps from the POV of the killer approaching a victim who recoils in terror. Another example can be seen in a second John Brahm–directed Laird Cregar feature, *Hangover Square* (1945), where the killer stabs a store clerk. This scene goes as far as to add the detail of an arm brandishing a knife swinging down in front of the camera lens, giving the sense that the arm is connected to the killer's torso in the position of the camera.

There is at the very least some association here between the audience and the killer, not only as we occupy their POV but also as they are our main character, and suspense is created in us about them being caught or unmasked as a killer. We see this suspense more from the killer's perspective than from that of the victims or detectives. Perhaps the movie that best captures the way in which the fear of being outed as killer mirrors the concerns of queer people being outed for their identities is the 1965 William Castle teen babysitter romp *I Saw What You Did*. In that film, teenagers Libby (Andi Garrett) and Kitt (Sara Lane) and Libby's kid sister Tess (Sharyl Locke) make prank phone calls to amuse themselves while home alone at night. At first, they call and pretend to be a sexy mistress named Suzette to stoke the ire of wives toward their husbands. It is an interesting choice as it already indicates that sexuality, particularly the tentative exploration of sexuality, is at play from the beginning of the phone game. They at some point in the evening switch to a more sinister prank call, whispering coyly, "I saw what you did . . . and I know who you are." One call reaches a man and woman kissing in bed illuminated only by a dim light through the windowpane. The man answers the phone and presumes the girls refer to his current sexual encounter. "You did?" he asks. "Nothing is sacred." A second nod to sexual voyeurism.

When they call Steve Marak (John Ireland), they at first get a particularly subdued response from his wife on the Suzette ruse. She seems not at all concerned about potential infidelities. When she goes into the shower to get him on the phone, she finds the room in shambles. She shouts at Steve through the shower door, "You wonder why I'm leaving you? You're not jealous. You're not that normal. You're insane!" He then pulls her into the shower and stabs her to death in a sequence that vividly recalls the shower scene in *Psycho*, including imitative shot compositions and editing techniques. Unable to get a response, the girls hang up. Meanwhile, Steve disposes of his wife's body. Later in the evening, the girls call back to prank him again and this time whisper, "I saw what you did . . . and I know who you are." Unlike the typical heteronormative implications of sexual indecency and extramarital affairs, Marek's call instigates paranoia about totally unexpected aspects of his identity that the teen girls do not, perhaps cannot, even conceive: Steve as murderer. Unlike the other men they call, Steve's life seems unmarked by heteronormative attitudes toward sex and romance. He is married but displays no emotion or affection for his wife, whom he murders. His neighbor, Amy (Joan Crawford), spends the film making romantic advances toward him that he coolly ignores. When he eventually murders her, he stands stone-faced while she desperately leans in to kiss him before falling to the floor, deceased. Having screened the film with a crowd, I can confirm the moment gets an uproarious, knowing laugh from both gay and straight audiences. Though Steve certainly inhabits a heteronormative world, he appears characteristically at odds with or indifferent to its pleasures.

Steve's noted disinterest in and detachment from heterosexuality, coupled with his immense anxiety over his mystery caller's discovery of a nonnormative identity, speaks to deeply held fears of being outed that are persistent in queer culture but especially potent in the film's more conservative time of release. More overtly queer films of the time such as *Victim* (Basil Dearden, 1961) and *The Children's Hour* (William Wyler, 1961) dramatized the persecution of gay characters via gossip and blackmail. *I Saw What You Did* ultimately reflects a desire to understand and distinguish individuals based on limiting discursive categories of identity—what Michel Foucault calls the "will to knowledge."[24] Such a desire is intimately linked to the invention of the homosexual as an identity category, after which the homosexual was, in Foucault's words, not just a person but also "a past, a case history, and a childhood . . . a secret that always gave itself away."[25]

Fig 1.3   Kit and Libby as shown in the opening shot of *I Saw What You Did* (1965) from the viewpoint of an uncertain set of eyes.

I Saw What You Did dramatizes a cultural desire to know secrets, investigate people's sexual interests and identities, and, very literally, *see* what they do and *know* who they are. The very first shot situates us as voyeurs while Libby and Kitt talk on the phone. Each character is enclosed within a respective almond-shaped "eye" frame. A perspective for the eyes is never established. We never know who is looking at them, besides us.

Cumulatively, this canon of preslasher films charts trends in style, plot, and theme that inform a richer history of the slasher and, more importantly, restore a queer history to the subgenre. It is certainly possible to make a slasher that does not engage with queerness. None of these traits is so indelible as to be unavoidable. Also, none of these traits works universally or in only one way. However, this history offers that the queer aspects of *Psycho* and the deviant sexuality and voyeurism of the slashers that followed were not without precedent earlier than 1960. The slasher as a subgenre is founded on tropes traceable back to at least the 1920s, and the queerness in these films goes back just as far. Reinstating this more comprehensive timeline helps us to understand the slasher's queer resonance to viewers, identifying that much of what came to be popular in the slasher is rooted in the depiction of queer characters and a queer dilemma of sexual difference.

PART TWO: QUEER FUNCTION

So, if the slasher has made queer people look like dangerous, sexually violent murderers for nearly one hundred years, what does it actually do *for* queer people? What can be salvaged from this history of murderous effeminate men and cross-dressing killers? Well, queerness is not a particularly safe or sterile political ideology. There is a lot of power in the brazen acts of vengeance that killers undertake in many of these films, and much of what they attack echoes those social structures queer people have politically opposed.

In particular, the political movement of gay liberation that followed the 1969 Stonewall uprising can be characterized as a movement of rebellion against the institutions depicted as targets of the slasher. Before this, the homophile movement led by earlier 1950s gay rights organizations such as Mattachine Society and Daughters of Bilitis had sought to remedy public perceptions of homosexuals as mentally ill and unequal to their straight peers. Early preslashers such as those described in this chapter offer substantial evidence of the period's popular myths about queer people, which treated gender and sexual differences as mental illness and conflated both with murderousness. Mattachine's group manifesto asked for the fair treatment of gay people with the expectation that they might convince straight America that "homosexuals can lead well-adjusted, wholesome, and socially productive lives."[26] While the homophile movement had the intention of making gay people a part of a straight society, gay liberation sought to refigure society outright. A 1971 statement by Third World Gay Liberation explicitly states "We want a new society" and proceeds to demand "a revolutionary socialist society" that opposes capitalism, the nuclear family, and organized religion by putting the needs of people first.[27] Gay Liberation Front, in its 1971 manifesto, similarly addresses contentions between homosexuals and family, psychiatry, the law, etc. The group expresses that "We intend to show you examples of the hatred and fear with which straight society relegates us to the position and treatment of sub-humans" and "We will show you how we can use our righteous anger to uproot the present oppressive system with its decaying and restrictive ideology . . . to form a new order, a liberated lifestyle."[28] These groups were unafraid to express their anger with institutions that policed their genders and sexualities and treated them as inferior.

In reckoning with the potential uses for more aggressive media that might seem to serve only volatile or destructive aims, I am reminded always of Audre Lorde's still vital distinction between hatred and anger in "The Uses of Anger." Hatred, she says, "is the fury of those who do not share our goals, and its object is death and destruction." Conversely, "anger is a grief of distortions between peers and its object is change."[29] Lorde's work here deals particularly with her frustrations as a Black lesbian over being characterized as "angry" when advocating for social change among her straight white peers. However, this construction speaks significantly to what a transformative politics of anger might look like. Most importantly, she makes clear that this revolutionary anger seeking change for the marginalized is in no way identical to the oppressive work of hatred embodied by racist and homophobic actions that harm marginalized communities. It is important to always keep this in mind when thinking about the revolutionary potential in seemingly aggressive works of art.

I argue that the slasher offers a potent site for the pleasurable dismantling of normative society through the visual metaphor of violence. For queer spectators, this is a comfortably rebellious feeling that echoes the sentiment of gay liberation to tear down the systems that oppress us and build a new world. The slasher visualizes a revolution-minded yet materially harmless attack on archetypal characters who stand in for those who were our bullies in high school: the cheerleader, the jock, the prom queen. A potentially queer appeal of the slasher is its iconoclastic disruption of normative teen narratives. It ruins the adoring applause of graduation day, sullies the glossy sheen of a vibrant summer camp. Ultimately, it embodies a dissonant stance against the complicit flow of normative society, and it does so with an exuberant glee. Queer pleasure can be found in the slasher's middle finger to everything we hate.

In his essay "Why I Love Violence," filth auteur John Waters suggests a queer function for violent representations that influences my perceptions here. While he avowedly means no physical harm to anyone, he describes a lifelong obsession with violence from a young age when he would play "car crash." Waters relays this obsession in a manner that implicitly reinforces its antinormative position. To be obsessed with violence is to work against the norms of comfort and safety. He is the only boy on the roller coaster disappointed when it does not combust. His pleasure refuses a system of norms by affectionately attaching to what repels others. Disgusted by a cultural obsession with sports, Waters maligns the normalcy of men asking him about local teams and presuming his interest based on perceived gender. He poses that he could just as easily enforce a demand for all men to provide insights into the latest Fassbinder film. He expresses this cultural resistance through fantasy violence most succinctly when he describes sardonically how he relishes an incident where an entire scout troop was "eaten by a berserk escalator on 'Scout Day'" at Memorial Stadium when it accidentally sped up to five times its speed and "began grinding up the little sports fans."[30]

Waters's joyfully obscene account of scouts—the proverbial benchmark for ordinary adolescence—being annihilated in the throes of sports adoration (an oppressive and detestable American pastime) echoes the slasher's work in giving audiences the

thrill of representationally chopping up schoolkids, camp coun-
selors, and prom queens. These paper-thin archetypes have so
little depth that popular critics and scholars have agreed we do
not care if they live or die. They are only a cavalcade of social
norms whereas the killer is commonly the most interesting character and point of interest for audiences. A 1986 *San Francisco
Chronicle* article describes *Silent Night, Deadly Night* (Charles E.
Sellier Jr., 1984) as "another teenage bloodbath movie where the
murderer, a lonely outsider, is the most sympathetic character in
the picture."[31] The article proceeds to describe with disgust the
acts of violence in the film, disappointedly recalling, "And the audience laughs."[32] A *New York Times* review of *Terror Train* (1980)
likewise describes the train full of teens as insubstantial characterizations, stating, "They are props, and you are unlikely to care
if one of them gets runs through with a saber or not."[33] In scholarship, Vera Dika describes the characters who populate the slasher
as "undistinguished, or nonspecific. They are dressed in clothes
that do not distinguish any particular style or trend . . . and most
all characters in the film are white, middle-class Americans."
She further gestures to the ways in which they signify less a real
group of individuals than a conceptual cross section of appealing
norms, stating that "these characters embody the America of the
print ad, of the television commercial."[34] It is important to clarify
that the slasher spectatorship described here does not advocate
for any form of violent action to be taken against other human
beings. In emphasizing this tradition of seeing the slasher as antihero and his victims as hapless stock characters we tend to root
against, I mean to make clear that for many audiences, watching
the slasher can be a potently queer experience, regardless of gender or sexuality, as the position of rooting for the queer outsider
and against the prom queen or jock uniquely treats all audiences
to an antinormative perspective.[35] More importantly, for queer
viewers there may be a profound reversal in the slasher where
a seemingly queer perspective (or at least one that resonates

with queer feelings) is suddenly made into what seems to be a dominant social experience. Running counter to all of the media wherein we are made to consume rhetoric centering the hetero-normative mating ritual that is prom, there is *Prom Night* (Paul Lynch, 1980), in which we get to watch it all be torn down. And the audience cheers.

In slashers, stock character types that reproduce oppressive gender norms have always been a major target. I would like to explore this by focusing on the exaggerated masculine arche-type of the "meathead" falling victim to the killer's violence. A behavior commonly ascribed to reckless male youth in slashers is the habitual need to prank peers, particularly other young men. A prominent demonstration of this can be seen in *The Burning*, which centrally exacerbates the meathead motif by situating the slasher as the victim of a summer camp prank gone wrong. When several boy campers at Camp Blackfoot decide to shock caretaker Cropsy (Lou David) with a worm-covered skull that has burning candles for eyes, he awakens suddenly, knocks the skull over, and runs from his cabin aflame. Seriously burned and scarred, Cropsy seeks vengeance by murdering the campers five years later. The majority of characters that populate the film (and die at the hands of Cropsy) satisfy Dika's account of being "undistinguished." In the idyllic milieu of the American summer camp, the characters engage in sports, sex, and malicious shenanigans. Boys particu-larly exhibit chauvinist tendencies in sexually pursuing girls and vie for superiority amongst their peers through pranks that seem to increase perceived social standing. These jocular antics render these characters expendable by associating them with grossly mundane masculinist behavior. The two characters that survive the film, Alfred (Brian Backer) and Todd (Brian Matthews), are portrayed as more sensitive and compassionate figures who fall victim to the system of pranks and scares that their peers use to assert dominance. Eventually, Todd is revealed to be one of the campers involved in the prank that burned Cropsy. His sensitive reflection on his past allows him to counsel Alfred about coping with social pressures. Alfred is notably awkward and confesses to being disliked and not having friends. In a scene in which Alfred reveals he is reluctant to swim, we see his male peers encouraging him not to "wuss out." A first-person camera shot then approaches Alfred from behind, shoving him into the water. It is revealed as the perspective of Glazer (Larry Joshua), who earlier taunted Alfred and called him a "little fucking weirdo." The shot mirrors the technique of first-person POV largely associated with the killer's approach of his victims, suggesting a similarity in their respective violence. Interestingly, in an earlier scene, Glazer threatens to "tear up" Alfred to the point where he is unrecognizable.

In addition to dramatizing the foolish hijinks of normative American boys (and disenchanting them with the introduction of violent danger), *The Burning* offers a particularly grim depiction of heterosexual sex. The camp's meatheads amount to a group of lechers, coercing women into a host of uncomfortable sexual encounters. In one particularly miserable indiscretion, Glazer brings Sally (Carrick Glenn) into the woods for sex. She expresses concern and discomfort, asking him to stop. She is told to "hold still," and following Glazer's premature ejaculation she asks, "That's all?" Even in situations not as forced and disappointing as this, scenes of heterosexual sex are still frequently used to connote an uncritical compliance with gender norms that makes their participants less likely to survive the night. In *Hell Night* (Tom DeSimone, 1981), four college pledges are left to fend for themselves overnight in a creepy old mansion. Marti (Linda Blair) and Jeff (Peter Barton) pair off and immediately get into a spat over her critique of his privileged upbringing in the wealthy community Hillsdale. She remarks that "the rich capitalist feeds on the life of the downtrodden poor," which prompts him to call her a "radical." In contrast to this, Seth (Vincent Van Patten) and May (Jenny Neumann) instantly produce Quaaludes and a flask and take to the bedroom. She asks him, "Don't you do anything but drink and screw?" to which he responds, "I surf." Both characters play off easy archetypes of party- and sex-obsessed college students. A running joke is that May, despite having sex with Seth multiples times, calls him by the wrong name throughout the film. Their coupling feels compulsory, as if it was the only thing two straight people could possibly do together. They are easily juxtaposed against the observant nature of Marti, who survives.[36]

Perhaps the singular most lucid takedown of the heteronormative jock/frat stereotypes represented and dismantled by these films is featured in *Happy Birthday to Me* (J. Lee Thompson, 1981). Greg (Richard Rebiere) is bench-pressing alone at night. An unknown figure dressed in black enters. Greg recognizes this figure and asks them to add more weights to his barbell. They oblige. He asks them to add more still. They oblige. The scene builds an expectation. Eventually the phantom figure will add too much weight. Greg will fall victim to his narcissistic need to impress with feats of strength. Finally, Greg does begin to struggle, and the weights become difficult for him to hold. He asks the figure to spot him, and they refuse. However, before Greg can succumb under the natural pressure of his barbell, the figure tosses a heavy weight on his crotch, causing Greg to recoil and drop the barbell onto his throat. What is most interesting here is the bait and switch attack on Greg's masculinity. The scene first invites a critique of the masculinist conduct of showing off one's physical strength, perhaps to a point of self-harm and excess. However, instead of resting on just that one blow to Greg's ego, it really delivers a death knell by straight up squashing his dick for good measure. It is a particularly vicious scene that works both as a slasher kill and as a visceral representation of a normative, meathead masculinity crushed.

In considering the historical circumstance of the slasher, which emerges in its commonly intelligible form in the mid- to late 1970s, it is important to recognize the parallel between its dramatization of contempt toward normative adolescent heterosexuality and

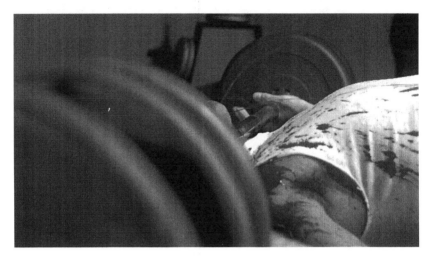

Fig 1.4 Bro, do you even lift? Greg in *Happy Birthday to Me* (1981) getting crushed under the weight of his own ambitions.

the early '70s gay liberation movement's critique of this culture. The Gay Liberation Front notes in its 1971 manifesto an ambition of obliterating societally enforced gender roles, a system that the slasher functionally mocks. As one of its primary aims, the Gay Liberation Front states that: "the long-term goal of Gay Liberation, which inevitably brings us into conflict with the institutionalised sexism of this society, is to rid society of the gender-role system which is at the root of our oppression. This can only be achieved by eliminating the social pressures on men and women to conform to narrowly defined gender roles. It is particularly important that children and young people be encouraged to develop their own talents and interests and to express their own individuality rather than act out stereotyped parts alien to their nature."[37] This language suggests an imperative need to rethink gender and avoid normative gender roles, particularly among young people. We are confronted with gender normativity in the slasher's sexually lecherous meatheads; the bad, futile sex they perpetuate; and the systematic mistreatment of women and other feminine people they sustain. By leaning on these profoundly one-dimensional archetypes of normative adolescence, the slasher creates a comfortable space to watch regressive ideas about gender and sexuality torn to shreds. This allows audiences to confront these norms and to pleasurably engage with their demise through the visual metaphor of violence.

While slashers have historically relied on queer stereotypes to denote murderousness in their killers, they simultaneously structure themselves as a strong critique of heteronormativity. This is seen in their quick dispatch of those who uphold a rigid gender role system, particularly those who espouse macho ideologies that devalue femininity. It is also present in the chosen settings for their attacks: the white suburbs of the Reagan 1980s and their representative sites of adolescent normativity, particularly rituals of heterosexuality, such as prom night and summer camp. The distilled queer essence of the slasher is perhaps this: A queer outsider ruins heterosexual bliss. The unique tension for queer audiences between seeing yourself represented as a killer and seeing the object of your oppression representatively killed is itself at the root of the duality in experience between queer people who love and hate slasher films. Neither stance is inaccurate, but each is receptive to different parts of the slasher formula, which are both true. These films are homophobic and transphobic, and yet, I argue, they are also resonantly queer.[38]

NOTES

1. For an overview of the canonical slasher's history and select filmography, see Richard Nowell, *Blood Money: A History of the First Teen Slasher Film Cycle* (New York: Continuum, 2011), Adam Rockoff, *Going to Pieces: The Rise and Fall of the Slasher Film, 1978–1986* (Jefferson, NC: McFarland, 2011), and Kent Byron Armstrong, *Slasher Films: An International Filmography, 1960 through 2001* (Jefferson, NC: McFarland, 2003).

2. These descriptions of the slasher draw on features outlined in Vera Dika, *Games of Terror: Halloween, Friday the 13th, and the Films of the Stalker Cycle* (Madison, NJ: Fairleigh Dickinson University Press, 1990)

and Carol J. Clover, *Men, Women, and Chain Saws: Gender in the Modern Horror Film* (Princeton, NJ: Princeton University Press, 1992). It should be noted that Dika is characterizing a subset of films she calls "stalker films," but all these films are included in the slasher subgenre.

3. Robin Wood, *Hollywood from Vietnam to Reagan* (New York: Columbia University Press, 1986), 195–201 and Clover, *Men, Women, and Chain Saws*, 40–42.

4. Important work on queer themes in the slasher include Harry Benshoff, "Satan Spawn and Out and Proud," in *Monsters in the Closet: Homosexuality and the Horror Film* (Manchester: Manchester University Press, 1997); Jack Halberstam, "Bodies That Splatter," in *Skin Shows: Gothic Horror and the Technology of Monsters* (Durham, NC: Duke University Press, 1995); Darren Elliott-Smith, "Gay Slasher Horror: Devil Daddies and Final Boys," in *Queer Horror Film and Television: Sexuality and Masculinity at the Margins* (London: I. B. Taurus, 2016); and A. L. Loudermilk, "Last to Leave the Theater: Sissy Spectatorship of Stalker Movies and the 'Final Girls' Who Survive Them," *Bright Lights Film Journal*, October 13, 2012, http://brightlightsfilm.com/last-to-leave-the-theater-sissy-spectatorship -of-stalker-movies-and-the-final-girls-who-survive-them.

5. See Michael Warner, "Introduction," in *Fear of a Queer Planet: Queer Politics and Social Theory* (Minneapolis: University of Minnesota Press, 1993); and Cathy J. Cohen, "Punks, Bulldaggers, and Welfare Queens: The Radical Potential of Queer Politics?" in *Sexual Identities, Queer Politics*, edited by Mark Blasius (Princeton, NJ: Princeton University Press, 2001).

6. Nowell, *Blood Money*, 111.

7. Dika, *Games of Terror*, 51–52 identifies *Halloween* as a postmodern variation on Alfred Hitchcock's 1960 film *Psycho*, noting that "much of this surface material has *skipped* a generation" and refers back to films of the late '50s and early '60s rather than films of the late '60s and early '70s. *Psycho* is also said to mark a major shift in Andrew Tudor, *Monsters and Mad Scientists: A Cultural History of the Horror Movie* (Oxford, UK, and Cambridge, MA: Basil Blackwell, 1989). Tudor describes the transition in 1960 as being from "secure" horror (which is monstrous and from outside the community) to "paranoid" horror (which is psychological and from within the community). These sources offer a sketch of how influence is commonly portrayed: *Psycho* is a moment of rupture, and *Halloween*, which gives rise to the slasher, is a strategic return to *Psycho*. I am posing instead a historical narrative of trends progressing across time that sees *Psycho* and *Halloween* within such a timeline.

8. See William Schoell, *Stay Out of the Shower: 25 Years of Shocker Films Beginning with "Psycho"* (New York: Dembner, 1985); and John Mc-Carty, *Movie Psychos and Madmen: Film Psychopaths from Jekyll and Hyde to Hannibal Lecter* (New York: Citadel, 1993).

9. Clover, *Men, Women, and Chain Saws*, 26–29 notably discusses the killer's expression of "gender distress."

10. For discussions of *Sleepaway Camp*'s uncertain presentation of Angela's gender, see Harmony M. Colangelo, "The Transgender Defense of Angela Baker and 'Sleepaway Camp,'" *Medium*, February 23, 2020, https://harmonycolangelo.medium.com/the-transgender-defense-of-angela-baker-and-sleepaway-camp-82dd54ddf9cd; and BJ Colangelo, "Going Back to *Sleepaway Camp*: Revisiting the Problematic Classic," *Dread Central*, June 5, 2019, https://www.dreadcentral.com/editorials/295274/going-back-to-sleepaway-camp-revisiting-the-problematic-classic.

11. Clover, *Men, Women, and Chain Saws*, 49.

12. Angela M. Smith, *Hideous Progeny: Disability, Eugenics, and Classic Horror Cinema* (New York: Columbia University Press, 2012).

13. A lot of this cultural mythology about domineering mothers ruining children can be found in World War II–era antifeminist literature admonishing women, especially for growth outside the home, such as Ferdinand Lundberg and Marynia F. Farnham, *Modern Woman: The Lost Sex* (New York: Harper and Brothers, 1947); and Patrick Wylie, *Generation of Vipers* (New York: Farrar and Rinehart, 1943).

14. For a history of Gein's crimes and their sensationalistic media coverage, see Harold Schechter, *Deviant: The Shocking True Story of Ed Gein, the Original Psycho* (New York: Pocket Books, 1989).

15. "House of Horror Stuns the Nation," *LIFE*, photographs by Francis Miller and Frank Scherschel, December 2, 1957, 24–32.

16. For a detailed study of Gein's influence on screen killers and a breakdown of the inconclusive factual evidence about his trans identity, see K. E. Sullivan, "Ed Gein and the Figure of the Transgender Serial Killer," *Jump Cut* 43 (2000): 38–47.

17. Joanne Meyerowitz, "Transforming Sex: Christine Jorgensen in the Postwar U.S." *Magazine of History* 20, no. 2 (March 2006): 16–20.

18. "Bars Marriage Permit: Clerk Rejects Proof of Sex of Christine Jorgensen," *New York Times*, April 4, 1959, 20; and "Engagement Off, Christine Is Told," *Washington Post*, September 9, 1959, D9.

19. The possible allusion to gender-affirming surgeries via the dialogue about Denmark is also observed in David Sanjek, "The Doll and the Whip:

Pathos and Ballyhoo in William Castle's *Homicidal*," *Quarterly Review of Film and Video* 20, no. 4 (2003): 259.

20. Ivor Novello appears in a sound remake of this film released in the US as *The Phantom Fiend* (Maurice Elvey, 1932), in which the lodger's twin brother (also Novello) turns out to be the killer.

21. The queer connotation of this speech is also described by Gregory Mank, *Laird Cregar: A Hollywood Tragedy* (Jefferson, NC: McFarland, 2019), 161.

22. Robin Wood offers a concise encapsulation of the Freudian thinking relevant to these films about the connection between repressed homosexuality and hatred of women in "The Murderous Gays," *Htichcock's Films Revisited* (New York: Columbia University Press, Revised Edition 2002), 336–40.

23. Clover, *Men, Women, and Chain Saws*, 186.

24. For an expanded discussion of this concept, see Jonathan Flatley, "Reading Into Henry James: Allegories of the Will to Know in *The Turn of the Screw*," in *Affective Mapping: Melancholia and the Politics of Modernism* (Cambridge, MA: Harvard University Press, 2008).

25. Michel Foucault, *The History of Sexuality, Volume 1: An Introduction*, trans. Robert Hurley (New York: Vintage, 1990), 43.

26. Harry Hay, *Radically Gay: Gay Liberation in the Words of Its Founder* (Boston: Beacon, 1996), 131.

27. Third World Gay Liberation (New York City), "What We Want, What We Believe," in *Out of the Closets: Voices of Gay Liberation*, edited by Karla Jay and Allen Young (New York: NYU Press, 1972), 367.

28. Gay Liberation Front, "Manifesto," published 1971, revised 1978, reprinted by Fordham University Internet History Sourcebooks Project, https://sourcebooks.fordham.edu/pwh/glf-london.asp.

29. Audre Lorde, *Sister Outsider: Essays and Speeches* (Toronto: Crossing, 2007), 129.

30. John Waters, *Shock Value: A Tasteful Book about Bad Taste* (New York: Running Press, 2005), 29.

31. Mick LaSalle, "'Silent Night' a Nasty Night at the Movies," *San Francisco Chronicle*, April 28, 1986, 56.

32. LaSalle, "'Silent Night' a Nasty Night at the Movies," 56.

33. John Corry, "Film: Spottiswoode's 'Terror Train': A Freshman's Revenge," *New York Times*, October 3, 1980, C10.

34. Dika, *Games of Terror*, 55–56.

35. Alexander Doty states that horror encourages queer positioning by all audiences because "much of it takes place within the space of the

contra-heterosexual and the contra-straight," in *Making Things Perfectly Queer: Interpreting Mass Culture* (Minneapolis: University of Minnesota Press, 1993), 15.

36. Clover, *Men, Women, and Chain Saws*, 40, discusses Marti as one of the final girls she describes as boyish, competent, and sexually reluctant.

37. Gay Liberation Front, "Manifesto."

38. Ideas and brief excerpts from this chapter also appear in *Recovering 1940s Horror Cinema: Traces of a Lost Decade*, eds. Mario DeGiglio-Bellemare, Charlie Ellbé, and Kristopher Woofter (Lanham, MD: Lexington, 2014), and *ReFocus: The Films of William Castle*, ed. Murray Leeder (Edinburgh: Edinburgh University Press, 2020).

WHAT EVER HAPPENED TO CHRISTMAS?

CHRISTMAS KILLS.

No really, it does.

If you don't believe me, just ask Barb from 1974's *Black Christmas*.

A scene for context.

Sitting alone in an eerily quiet sorority house, Jess (Olivia Hussey), awaits a call from a heavy-breathing murderer, hoping that this time it can be tracked by the police. She does not yet know the suffocated body of Clare (Lynne Griffin) remains in the attic with a plastic bag over her head, mouth frozen agape. However, the film cuts to a shot of the body to remind us of this threat. The first-person camera establishes the mobile perspective of the lurking killer within the house as he climbs down from the attic and hovers over the sleeping Barb (Margot Kidder), seeming to imply that she will be his next victim. The film cuts back to Jess tensely fidgeting with her hands as she waits. We hear a deep, blood-curdling gasp for breath, as if someone is being strangled. Jess opens the door to Barb's room. We are shown this action from behind the headboard of Barb's bed, leaving her body in relative darkness with only the silhouette of Jess clearly visible in the doorway. Jess flicks on the light, and in a moment of misdirection, Barb is not being strangled at all but merely coughing in her sleep. Jess helps her locate and use her inhaler. We see the end of this scene from the first-person camera perspective of the killer just outside the door, now watching Jess on the bed talking to Barb. He drifts away from the room and moves down the hall, leaving the two of them alone. Perhaps the threat has been evaded?

Enter Christmas . . . and children.

As Barb's asthma symptoms are relieved, Jess's attention is drawn to the sound of faint, sweet singing. Smash cut to a row of singing children with the sort of expressionless faces and singsong cadence that are hallmarks of milquetoast temperaments with conformist ambition. I was raised in Catholic schools, and their cold, dead eyes signal to me something vividly real about that experience. You find yourself lined up alphabetically or by height or birthday, standing with other children in identical uniforms, and when prompted you expel preprogrammed greetings with sing-song precision: "Gooood afternoooon, Sister Kathleeeeeen." And if you venture afoul, you're punished. I digress. Jess peeks out the window. She's thrilled. Singing children! It's Christmas!

We watch her watch them sing.

But wait! Something else.

As they sing, the first-person killer/camera returns. The killer walks back down the hall toward Barb's room. The two events are now linked through parallel editing, alternating between shots of Barb's impending murder and Jess, ignorant of the murder, watching the Christmas carolers. The killer/camera notices a glass statue above Barb's bed, a unicorn with a sharp horn. I don't know if I have the audacity to suggest that there is something innately queer about it being a unicorn, but it certainly doesn't hurt, does it? As the killer lowers the unicorn horn and brutally stabs Barb to death, the jabs are intercut with close-ups of the singing children. They follow in quick succession. A jab of the

Fig 2.1 The extremely ghoulish, sullen faces of Christmas carolers at the door in *Black Christmas* (1974).

unicorn. A close-up of a singing child's face. Again, and again. The pattern suggests a kind of buildup where the increasingly harsh and graphic violence brings us into even nearer proximity with the singing children, down to an extreme close-up of just a pair of singing lips. The scene concludes with a dark joke in which Jess applauds at the end of the carol followed by a cut to Barb's bloody hand as it falls, indicating her death. The applause feels like it's as much for the performance of murder as it is for the children's singing.

On the surface, I suppose, we can see this juxtaposition as a form of irony, contrasting a rather stereotypical embodiment of innocence and purity with something bleak and painfully mortal. But this feels too easy, and, more importantly, the scene itself invites us into a perspective that does not take the culturally constructed innocence of the carolers seriously. It has Jess applaud at the end of the murder, and it presents us with such starkly sullen singing faces, pushing in closer and closer until they feel surreal and creepy. It also sets up the scene so that the carolers' arrival disrupts the possibility for safety and creates the distraction that facilitates Barb's murder. There seems to be a grim sense of humor here, one that allows for murder to be painful and brutal but also situates the murder in a way that undermines the pristine, superficial presentation of the Christmas holiday. I'm inclined to interpret the scene as a macabre joke, one that demonstrates how facile death is in the slasher and how much the slasher's kills mark disruptions of socially normative rituals.[1] In chapter 1, I described how the slasher symbolically destroys characters and settings that represent white heteronormative bourgeois society. In this chapter, I will add to my argument by articulating an important reoccurring pattern within this framework: the slasher as anti-Christmas or ruining Christmas. I suggest there is a distinctly queer politics to ruining Christmas. By exploring different queer relationships with Christmas, this chapter will explain how diversifying the meaning of Christmas resists a monolithic understanding of the holiday, a practice enmeshed with the queer history of diverse experiences with gender and sexuality that do not conform to traditional cisgender and heterosexual norms. I further explore how the slasher's emergence in the 1970s runs parallel to developing queer independent cinema and suggest that the slasher's independent production history and counter-cultural themes can be better understood when seen alongside queer cinema of the time rather than exclusively other horror cinema. These two threads of the chapter come together in a final reading of the low-budget slasher *Silent Night, Bloody Night* (Theodore Gershuny, 1972), which both disrupts Christmas and shares connections with 1970s independent queer cinema, notably Andy Warhol's Factory.

PART ONE: QUEERING CHRISTMAS

To fully explore what makes the scene above an effectively queer critique, I'd like to consider some of the foundational queer perspectives that inform this interpretation. To begin, I will reiterate the queer politics of the gay liberation movement described in chapter 1. Notably, that following the Stonewall uprising in 1969, gay rights organizations sought to refigure society at large rather than assimilate into it, which had been a leading philosophy of the more subordinate 1950s homophile movement. The politics of gay liberation, which historically parallel the slasher's development in the '70s, identified the law, the media, the church, and the nuclear family as oppressive structures to queer people that needed to be actively resisted and reformed.[2] Eve Kosofsky Sedgwick offers us a remarkable articulation of how Christmas represents a major collaboration between all these oppressive forces.

> The depressing thing about the Christmas season—isn't it?—is that it's the time when all of the institutions are speaking with one voice. The Church says what the Church says. But the State says the same thing: maybe not (in some ways it hardly matters) in the language of theology, but in the language the State talks: legal holidays, long school hiatus, special postage stamps, and all. And the language of commerce more than chimes in, as consumer purchasing is organized ever more narrowly around the final weeks of the calendar year, the Dow Jones aquiver over Americans' "holiday mood." The media, in turn, fall in triumphally behind the Christmas phalanx: ad swollen magazines have oozing turkeys on the cover, while for the news industry every question turns into the Christmas question—Will hostages be free *for Christmas*? What did the flash flood or mass murder (umpty-ump people killed and maimed) do to those families' *Christmas*? And meanwhile, the pairing "families/Christmas" becomes increasingly tautological, as families more and more constitute themselves according to the schedule, and in the endlessly iterated image, of the holiday itself constituted in the image of "the" family.[3]

Sedgwick instead offers that *queer* should refer to the possibility for enmeshed and overlapping meanings. That where normativity seeks to make things "line up" in a neat and orderly fashion, queerness seeks to explore those places where things don't line up. In queer identity and social experience, this can commonly be seen, as Sedgwick describes, in a queer reimagining of combinations of gender identity and sexual attraction such that the idea that one's gender should correspond with their assigned sex at birth and that they should seek a partner of a different gender who also identifies with their assigned sex at birth would no longer be standard behavior. Queer possibilities allow for trans and nonbinary identities, variety in partner identities, and myriad combinations of sexual behaviors and identities, and in doing so they set a course for a queer politics resistant to normative traditions. Moreover, *queer* offers a way to describe the political potential of resistance toward monolithic singularity in meaning, which Sedgwick articulates through Christmas. Whereas a normative understanding of Christmas seeks this "lining up" of Christmas with church, family, media, and state, a queer reimagining might challenge that illusion of oneness. As Sedgwick poses, "What if instead there was a practice for valuing the ways in which meanings and institutions can be at loose ends with each other? What if the richest junctures weren't the ones where everything means the same thing?"[4]

I argue that scenes such as the one I began with from *Black Christmas* offer us a queer experience of Christmas specifically because they do not reaffirm the traditional associations of Christmas iconography. Rather than offering the warm, fuzzy feeling we see affirmed in other Christmas media, they create new possibilities and associations for Christmas and its popular imagery. The scene achieves this very deliberately through parallel editing that formally stitches together the imagery of children singing Christmas carols with images of a brutal and violent murder. It makes the images inextricable from each other and, through cross-cutting, forges a new association that radically departs from tradition. Rather than associating carolers with wholesome Christmas themes such as family and religion, we instead see the new possibility of violence and murder introduced. Breaking from traditional associations creates for me the kind of opportunity Sedgwick poses to see things not "line up" or "mean the same thing." Through their careful dissection of Christmas iconography and their reassociation of Christmas imagery with unexpected feelings, Christmas slashers forge queer multiplicities of meaning. Allowing for more and new experiences with Christmas feels importantly queer on its own. And yet, opening up experiences with Christmas specifically to trauma feels especially queer. Speaking personally as the queer child of a conservative Catholic family who is still to this day sometimes cajoled to return home for the occasion, I feel associating Christmas with trauma is an especially accurate affirmation of my annual encounter with the holiday, and I feel certain I am not alone among queers in having this experience.

I additionally locate the queer history for such associations in the work of filmmaker John Waters, who has reflected on the holiday in interviews, in holiday-themed speaking tours, and in his essay "Why I Love Christmas" from the book *Crackpot*. An especially apropos anecdote from that essay finds Waters reflecting nostalgically on the cherished childhood memory of his family arriving at his grandmother's house only to find that a fully decorated Christmas tree had tipped over and pinned her to the ground. Waters recounts with glee that he sang "O Christmas Tree! O Christmas Tree!" while his parents tried to free her from the weight of the tipped tree.[5] As with Waters's anecdote of playing "car crash" discussed in chapter 1, there is a departure here from a conventional expectation that presumes the desired outcome of any experience to be safety. Waters expresses a queer sensibility through his retooled engagement with conventionally unattractive concepts like violence and filth. We see this in his film work through the screen persona of drag queen Divine, who in the queer classic *Pink Flamingos* (1972) competes with Connie Marble (Mink Stole) for the title of "filthiest person alive," culminating in the infamous scene where Divine eats dog shit off the sidewalk in Baltimore (shot in one continuous take to assure verisimilitude). Coveting filth, violence, and death eschews the normative impulse to, in Sedgwick's terms, make things "line up." It instead distinctly emphasizes perversions that resonate with a queer refusal of normativity and celebrates disorder and difference. Elsewhere, Waters describes perverse holiday traditions such as gathering Black and effeminate homosexual friends to go caroling in "*Father Knows Best*-type" white suburban neighborhoods and replacing the face of the baby Jesus with Charles Manson on greeting cards ("He is born").[6] He says, "The best thing to do is get Hallmark cards and deface them! Change them to say, 'Season's Beatings,' you know? I'm really into taking the traditional Christmas and twisting it."[7] Key to each of these is an emphasis on rupturing the conventional associations of Christmas iconography and reassociating the holiday and its imagery with something depraved, sexual, violent, or otherwise different from the norm. As with the scene from *Black Christmas*, Christmas in these queer terms allows for different experiences rather than only one culturally reaffirmed monolithic experience. But, most importantly, the variations these subversions commonly emphasize avow trauma as a possible outcome of Christmas, a recognition that I feel speaks especially to queer experiences.

I settled on the word *trauma* as an appropriate expression of the unconventional association with Christmas that most speaks to queer encounters with the holiday largely due to the influence of *The Jinkx and DeLa Holiday Special*, a scripted film version of a touring show by drag performers Jinkx Monsoon and Ben-DeLaCreme created by necessity when the COVID-19 pandemic sidelined their annual tour in 2020. In it, BenDeLaCreme, a cock-eyed optimist character, tries desperately to re-create the magic of her childhood Christmas. She even resorts to speaking with the ghost of her nana, who possesses a particularly festive glass of eggnog. Meanwhile, the notably more cynical and pagan booze-hound character Monsoon bemoans the holiday and seeks to deter DeLa's pursuit of traditional holiday cheer. Together they find a comfortable middle ground as DeLa comes to remember the holiday with less nostalgia and as one more accurately marred by passive aggressive family dinners and drunken racist relatives. Meanwhile, Monsoon agrees to work together with the disappointed DeLa to forge new Christmas traditions that reflect their lived experiences as queer artists and performers. In a climactic song and dance number entitled "Everyone Is Traumatized by Christmas," the pair delivers a jolly but ultimately quite cynical take that skewers the holiday's common traditions (evoking, for example, the perversion of putting children on so many strange men's laps because they are "Santa") while also evoking a universal queer feeling of discontentment with the holiday. I like especially this idea that everyone is traumatized by Christmas rather than warmed, or comforted, or made jolly, specifically because it recalls Waters's suggestions that traditional Christmas might be given a "twist," often through the invocation of sex or violence, to create the possibility for alternative experiences of the holiday that disturb the monolith. Interestingly, and I think very importantly, the song expands on the universality of Christmas trauma by exclaiming not only that the queer speakers of the song are traumatized by Christmas but that—as in the title—*everyone* is traumatized by Christmas. This move makes a careful choice to reach a wider audience and to acknowledge that traumatic associations with Christmas need not line up neatly along a divide between straight and queer or cis and trans audiences. If, in fact, a queer viewer has DeLa's warm memories, perhaps indeed they were not only traumatized but sometimes actually comforted by Christmas. And straight cis audiences, perhaps even the most conservatively affirmed by the monolith of Christmas, might indeed acknowledge that at least in some form or at some time, Christmas did not feel only one way, and perhaps trauma was one way among many that it may have felt. The importance here is that a queer version of Christmas is not truly or purely anti-Christmas and does not only invite negative experiences with the holiday but instead acknowledges, as Sedgwick does, that the richest junctures are those where not everything means the same thing. By recalibrating Christmas iconography through associations with violence and trauma, these media acknowledge other possibilities of feeling about a holiday uniformly depicted as wholesome, sexless, white, middle-class, cisgender, and heterosexual. In these moments of Christmas trauma, we can see that there is more than only one way of being in Christmas—and everything else.

With these perspectives in mind, I would like to approach the subject of Christmas slashers—a subset of the slasher subgenre that makes use of the Christmas season as a backdrop for carnage. The association of trauma with Christmas iconography underlies much of the Christmas slasher's purpose. With titles like *Black Christmas; Christmas Evil; Silent Night, Deadly Night; Silent Night, Bloody Night;* and *To All a Goodnight,* these films tend to reframe seemingly banal expressions of the holiday into threats and to especially focus on transforming the peaceful associations with the central phrase *silent night.* The obvious move here is that in the realm of the slasher, a seemingly peaceful evening in a heteronormative white, affluent suburban community will be disrupted by an outsider—the killer. The titles especially like to undermine the traditional pairing of *silent night* and *holy night* from the classic carol and instead offer a rotten alternative: *bloody, deadly,* or *evil* night.[8]

Childhood trauma set in the shadow of the Christmas holiday and continually associated with Christmas iconography forms the foundations for many of these films. For example, *Christmas Evil* (Lewis Jackson, 1980) opens with a childhood flashback of the protagonist, Harry (Gus Salud), sneaking downstairs to spy on Santa Claus. What he sees is his father in a Santa costume in a private sexual encounter with his mother. The scene plays like a perverse restaging of the popular Christmas song "I Saw Mommy

Kissing Santa Claus," in which the speaker of the song recounts seeing his mother kissing Santa underneath the mistletoe, not knowing it is really his father in a Santa costume. Harry then bolts up the stairs, seemingly in a state of distress. He picks up a Christmas snow globe and smashes it on the floor. This action is intercut with images of Santa's hand running up Harry's mother's leg and other erotic moments from the prior scene. We see Harry take the shards of glass from the floor and use them to slice open his hand. The sequence cements a recalibration of Christmas imagery that informs the rest of the film. Harry's previously jovial childhood interaction with Santa is now reshaped into a site of childhood trauma. Following a credits sequence, we meet Harry again years later, played by Brandon Maggart, and find that he has developed into a Santa-obsessed adult. His home is filled to the brim with tchotchkes displaying the jolly bearded man. Moreover, Harry demonstrates an increasing need to see himself as a Santa. This is signaled early in the film during a scene in which he sculpts shaving cream on his face into the shape of a bushy white beard and seems to take pleasure from it. In a DVD commentary for the film, John Waters describes this phenomenon as a full-blown "Santa fetish."[9] The perverse connotation of Harry's obsession with being Santa extends to creepy scenes in which he watches children through binoculars and determines whether the behavior he spies is naughty or nice. To fulfill his wish of being Santa, Harry keeps detailed records of all the neighborhood children's behavior and inappropriately surveils their lives. As in "Everyone Is Traumatized by Christmas," where putting children on strange men's laps is evoked as a grim but socially normalized practice of the holiday with potentially dangerous implications, Christmas Evil picks up on obscene features of the Santa myth and reinforces for viewers how disturbing a figure Santa would be if real. We see this in Harry's surveillance of minors, his nighttime break-ins to family homes, and his "sleigh" (a van with connotations of child abduction). This potentially catastrophic depiction of the Santa myth emphasizes the willfully obtuse perception of the holiday by many as wholesome. In plainest terms, without the cultural halo of innocence, these behaviors feel stark, upsetting, and pedophilic.

A very similar narrative of Christmas trauma belongs to Billy in *Silent Night, Deadly Night* (Charles E. Sellier Jr., 1984). In an opening sequence, young Billy (Jonathan Best) witnesses his parents being murdered by a killer in a Santa suit. Prior to the murders, Billy has an unnerving encounter with his grandfather at a home for seniors. The seemingly nonresponsive grandpa, having been totally still and silent during the family visit, becomes alert when left alone with Billy and begins explaining to him in a menacing voice that Christmas Eve is the scariest night of the year because Santa will only bring gifts to those that have been good and will punish those who have been naughty. The exchange has an abusive undertone and echoes a bleak concern about what happens to children when left alone with adults. In this private moment, Billy gains access to a side of his grandfather not visible to his family, and this knowledge transforms his relationship with the Santa myth into one of terror. Billy recounts this conversation on the car ride home, explaining that he no longer wants Santa to visit because he fears punishment. When Billy's mother exclaims that his grandfather is "nothing but a crazy old fool," Billy tells her she is being naughty and will be punished by Santa. He sees Grandpa's warning as being fulfilled when a man dressed as Santa murders her. Years later, in a convent-operated school for orphaned children, Billy (Danny Wagner) is sent by his teacher to the office of the Mother Superior (Lilyan Chauvin) after he draws a Christmas scene filled with blood and gore that repels his classmates. Billy's infraction of etiquette here is his revelation of an alternative view of Christmas defined by the past trauma of his parents' murders.

After the Mother Superior scolds Billy for representing his different view of the Christmas holiday, we transition to another scene in which a second infraction of etiquette draws even more anger. Mother Superior spies Billy in the hallway peering through a keyhole at two teenagers engaged in a sexual encounter. Mother Superior pushes Billy aside and forces her way into the room, scolding the teenagers and beating them with a belt as punishment. Mother Superior then locates Billy on the playground where he is helping schoolmates build a snowman. She tells him that the teenagers having sex were being naughty, that people who are naughty get punished, and that "punishment is good." We then endure a painful low-angle shot from beneath Billy as he is bent across a chair and beaten by Mother Superior's belt. Mother Superior's child abuse climaxes in a final confrontation where she makes the premeditated decision to force the terrified Billy to sit on Santa's lap despite knowing his negative associations with the character. This results in Billy punching the orphanage Santa in the face before cowering in the corner awaiting his punishment.

Billy's childhood abuse further solidifies the association between Christmas and violence that ultimately leads him to become another killer in a Santa suit. As an adult, he gets a job at a toy store during the holiday season and is eventually made a last-minute replacement for an injured store Santa. Once he dons Santa's white beard and red suit, his traumatic associations with the holiday become maximally provoked, which manifests in a murder spree. The subsequent murder scenes function as a critique of Catholicism's history of corporal punishment and the punitive ideology enmeshed in the Santa myth, both of which play roles in forging Billy's killer psychology. We see the hypocritical approach to violence taken by Mother Superior when she scolds Billy for his expression of violent trauma in his drawing but then immediately contradicts this with her own abusive violence in her punishments. Though the cathartic and expressive relationship with violence seen in Billy's artwork is deemed taboo and inappropriate, Mother Superior's punitive violence is deemed good. This builds on what Billy learned from his grandpa and the killer Santa who murdered his parents about how people who are naughty will be punished by Santa. Billy, as Santa, will go on to kill those whom he sees as naughty, conflating his mother's killer dressed as Santa with the popular Santa myth and Mother Superior's own violent punishments.

Mother Superior's abuse also develops aspects of sexual repression and sexual trauma instilled in Billy by his mother's murder, which involved her blouse being torn open to expose her bare breasts during a sexual assault. This conflation of violent punishment with sexuality becomes reinforced by the beating of the teenagers Billy sees having sex in the orphanage. The film establishes adult Billy's sexual trauma (his view of sex as naughty and in need of punishment) during a dream in which we see him having sex with a coworker before getting stabbed by a Santa Claus. After jolting awake with fright, Billy cowers in the fetal position at the corner of the room, emotionally reassuring himself aloud that "I want to be good."

I find this moment painfully familiar. As a queer child raised in a conservative Catholic family and educated in Catholic schools, queer sexualities and gender nonconforming behaviors were typically sites of reinforced shame. In Billy's moment of being blindsided by the outrage of the teacher over his drawing, I'm reminded of many childhood memories where I was scolded for things I did not understand. I realize now these were moments of gender nonconformism being reined in. They were attempts to reinforce negative associations with dolls, with pink frosted cupcakes, with hair scrunchies that I wasn't supposed to want or have. And in those confusing moments, I learned instead to be unnecessarily cautious about self-expression, worrying that any revelation of myself would trigger anger that I could not reliably anticipate. In Billy's assertion that he wants "to be good," I'm reminded of an assembly at my Catholic high school where a priest alleged that if we were gay, we could *still* be loved by God if we never had queer sex, if we avoided partnership and denied ourselves pleasure. I remember sitting there and finding that a perfectly reasonable and logical loophole. And feeling hope. That I had a chance still. If I just did nothing. I wanted to be good, like Billy. The scenes of trauma in *Silent Night, Deadly Night* may play any number of ways to any number of people, but I can see them only as resonating with my own and others' queer experiences. They acknowledge aspects of the Catholic church's hypocritical punitive violence and hateful compulsion to convert, to suppress unpleasant deviations from the norm in favor of monolithic singularity.

Upon the release of *Silent Night, Deadly Night,* parents freaked out about the idea of a killer dressed as Santa because this imagery challenged commonly professed narratives of family Christmas. These differently oriented Christmas images were also met with a moral imperative to shame those involved in perpetuating them. In an infamous episode of the movie review show *At the Movies,* hosted by Gene Siskel and Roger Ebert, Siskel pointedly names the distributing studio, TriStar Pictures, along with all its financial partners on the film and rebukes them, saying, "Shame on you." He then proceeds to name the film's creative talents, including gay producer Ira Barmak, telling them, "You people have nothing to be proud of. . . . Your profits truly are blood money."[10] The episode followed public protests of the film, including the picketing of theaters by a Milwaukee group called Citizens Against Movie Madness, which succeeded in prematurely ending the film's run in at least three local theaters.[11] TriStar Pictures announced after its first week of television advertisements that they were pulling ads for the film from circulation.[12] Mike Davis, programming director of WTTV-TV in Indianapolis, summed up the complaints about the television ads for *Silent Night, Deadly Night* like this: "We had a lot of people saying they were upset that their children tuned into a family show and saw a new version of Santa Claus."[13] Davis's remarks highlight that the overwhelming problem reported was a conflict of meaning, that families expected a certain singularity of meaning around the image of Santa to be preserved, and the advertisements instead exposed children to a "new version of Santa." The fear appears to be that such variety of meaning would confuse the central narrative that families and traditional Christmas media deliver to children.

The standardization of meaning around Santa Claus functions as a key point of suspense and danger in *Christmas Evil* and *Silent Night, Deadly Night*. Both films depict scenes in which unwitting children, having been taught only the narrative of Santa as friendly and jolly, simply do not understand that Santa could do anything to hurt them. In *Christmas Evil*, a group of parents watch in fear as their children run up to greet Harry, dressed as Santa. Television news stories detailing Harry's murders have alerted parents to the dangerous Santa. One father pulls out a knife, and the group of children cling tightly to Harry, forming a barricade to protect him from their own parents. A little girl emerges from the pack, clings to her father's leg, and gets him to drop his knife. She then picks the knife up and delivers it to Harry with a smile. In *Silent Night, Deadly Night*, Mother Superior sits huddled with a room full of children in the orphanage, having heard that Billy might be on his way there. Despite efforts to lock everyone in for safety, a boy happily opens the door for Billy, who is dressed as Santa. When Mother Superior tries to warn the children to stay away from him, a girl remarks, "But Mother Superior, it's Santa Claus," as if there could be no other outcome from greeting Santa besides cheer and presents. Both scenes emphasize the dangers of enforced naivete, of creating a singularity of meaning that renders children helpless and submissive to any man in a red suit and white beard. They play on the horrors of child abuse and implicate parents in the vulnerability of their own children, a vulnerability that might be softened if children were offered more nuanced information and not shielded from multiplicities of meaning regarding Christmas imagery.[14]

The slasher's disruption of heteronormative representations of Christmas provides one way to consider its queerness. Making a mockery of family Christmas takes form not just in Christmas slashers but also in representative examples of 1970s independent queer cinema. John Waters's independent sleaze classic *Female Trouble*, in which Dawn Davenport (played by drag queen Divine) is executed for murder, was released in 1974, the same year as Tobe Hooper's *The Texas Chainsaw Massacre*, an independent sleaze classic of a different sort in which gender nonconforming killer Leatherface (Gunnar Hansen) kills a group of friends who stop for gas. This is also the same year as Bob Clark's *Black Christmas*, initially financed and released in Canada before being distributed by Warner Bros. in the United States as *Silent Night, Evil Night*. Acknowledging these historical congruences is not meant to suggest an innate relation between such titles but instead hopefully clarifies my own understanding of the slasher as meaningfully parallel in style and theme with independent queer cinema of its time, a context it is not often considered alongside.

Compare the image of Divine as Dawn Davenport, scarred by acid, with a prosthetic mask of facial scars beneath caked on makeup, alongside the image of Leatherface with a mop of black hair, rouged cheeks, and blue eyeshadow adorning the sockets of his human flesh mask. Side by side, the two evoke a common spirit of gender nonconformism and a radical antagonism toward social norms and conservative attitudes. They are vanguards of chaotic refusals to conform, and their nonconformism is expressed through gender difference, alternative concepts of glamour, and a reckless violence that discomforts society. In chapter 1, I discussed how Waters's playacting fantasies of violence can be understood as manifesting a queer sensibility. In *Female Trouble*, we see the extension of this oddity to theories of beauty and appearance. In the moment of Dawn's facial burn by acid, Donald Dasher (David Lochary) and Donna Dasher (Mary Vivian Pearce), the voyeuristic couple who have hired her to be their "crime model" and let them photograph her depravity, approach with frenzied enthusiasm to take pictures of her gorgeous acid-burned face. They discourage the doctor's recommendation for Dawn to see a plastic surgeon and insist instead she will "now be more beautiful than if she had a million-dollar facelift." Dawn learns to accept this alternative definition of beauty. In an iconic scene, she dances confidently to the song "Dig" by Nervous Norvus in a leopard print dress, proudly modeling her acid-burned face for passersby. We see a close-up of one man watching aghast as his prosthetic eye bursts from its socket and falls out of frame. The gawking scene recalls (and subverts) a similar moment from *The Girl Can't Help It* (Frank Tashlin, 1956) in which prototypical Hollywood glamour star Jayne Mansfield makes her entrance sauntering down the street to the Little Richard title tune of the film with onlookers performing hyperbolic gestures that visualize their attraction.[15] This includes a milkman whose bottle of milk pops its lid and overflows in a paper-thin nod to ejaculation at the sight of Mansfield. Dawn's acceptance of new forms of physical beauty is framed as a step on her path toward radicalization, which culminates with an audacious stage performance in which she delivers a speech about her depraved behavior, including "I blew Richard Speck," and then asks, "Who wants to die for art?" before firing live rounds into the crowd, murdering members of her audience.

The first steps in Dawn's radicalization take shape in a disturbance of family Christmas not altogether unlike the inciting traumas that start off many Christmas slashers. At school, Dawn is chastised by the teachers and preppy college-bound girls for being poor and fat. She is made to write "I will not eat in class"

Fig 2.2–2.3 A study in rebellious carnage. The stitched and sewn visage of Leatherface in *The Texas Chainsaw Massacre* (1974) and the acid-burned face of Dawn Davenport caked with makeup in *Female Trouble* (1974).

on the blackboard after a bratty girl tells on her for eating a meatball sandwich. Her friends at school all smoke in the bathroom and get in trouble for violating the conservative dress code. On Christmas, Dawn reluctantly joins in a family chorus of "Silent Night," eagerly hoping her parents will give her the cha-cha heels she demanded as a gift. When she opens her present, she is disappointed to learn they failed her. Moreover, the failure is not a misunderstanding but a moral judgment because, as her father says, "Nice girls don't wear cha-cha heals." A furious Dawn hurls the present across the room and pushes over the family Christmas tree on top of her mother, who murmurs, "Not on Christmas."[16] Dawn storms out of the house, shouting, "I hate Christmas." She begins hitchhiking and is picked up by Earl Peterson, played by Divine out of drag, with whom she has sex in public on a discarded mattress. Months later, Dawn gives birth to their daughter, Taffy, alone on a sofa. She tears the umbilical cord with her teeth. This unconventional family narrative expands to years of belligerent hostility between Dawn and Taffy (Mink Stole). Later, when Dawn becomes enamored with hairdresser Gater (Michael Potter), he casually remarks that Taffy should "come suck your daddy's dick." When Taffy finally becomes fed up with this mistreatment by Dawn and Gater, she sets out to find her "real" dad, calling on Earl Peterson, an equally disappointing drunk who vomits on her and exposes his penis in a lewd sexual advance.

Nuclear families have a putrid lineage of repeating abusive patterns throughout *Female Trouble*, particularly among fathers and paternal figures. We see a comparably decrepit patriarchal legacy at work in *The Texas Chainsaw Massacre* through the figure of Grandpa (John Duggan). In the film, a displaced family of slaughterhouse workers whose labor has been automated by modern technology take to cannibalism and process human flesh like the parts of animals, using it for food, clothing, and furniture. Sally (Marilyn Burns) is the last of a group of friends to survive being captured by the family and is set up at the dinner table to be killed by Grandpa. The family of cannibal killers clap and chant with glee at the excitement to see Grandpa kill, as he is "the best." Grandpa is actually an emaciated, corpse-like husk of a man with pale white skin. He barely seems alive, let alone a virile killer. As the family cheers for Grandpa, they position Sally's head over a bucket to be smashed with a hammer. However, Grandpa is so immobile, he continually drops the hammer. Each time, the family picks it up and futilely replaces it in his hand. Eventually, they adopt a hand-over-hand approach to put Grandpa through the motions and preserve their fantasy of his skill and power. It's a sad display of killer impotence that underscores not only that the morally bankrupt family of killers have lost their way but that their desperate attempts to hold onto patriarchy is ultimately the hollow worship of a flaccid figurehead. Robin Wood describes *Chainsaw Massacre*'s cannibal family as the horrific evolution of the US family comedy. He calls classical Hollywood family films, such as *Meet Me in St. Louis* (Vincente Minnelli, 1944), "comedy of containment" that allows us to laugh at the horrors of family life to help us see them as "acceptable" and "affectionate." Whereas "by the 1970s such containment is no longer possible, though ideology continues to repress the imagining of constitutive social alternatives."[17] Thus making *Texas Chainsaw* a "comedy of despair" defined by hopelessness.

As I expressed at the start of this chapter and previously in chapter 1, the period of gay liberation politics following Stonewall named the heterosexual nuclear family as a concept that needed dismantling along with oppressive structures such as psychiatry, the law, and the church. The gestures here to failed family dynamics rotted from the inside out reflect the queer political imperatives of their respective times. Moreover, in the figure of the radicalized and gender nonconforming killer, Leatherface and Divine, we have a fascinating avatar for queer anger against heteronormativity. As Aunt Ida (Edith Massey) famously laments in *Female Trouble*, "the world of heterosexuals is a sick and boring life."

It's also a time in which queer people are still contending with institutional policing of their sexuality. Antisodomy laws were stricken from state law books on a case-by-case basis, but many queer people continued to be harassed and arrested for private sex acts and gender nonconforming expressions. A federal precedent by the US Supreme Court establishing that such laws were unconstitutional did not come until 2003's *Lawrence v. Texas*, overturning the 1986 decision of *Bowers v. Hardwick*, which had upheld antisodomy laws as constitutional.[18] It was not until 1973 that the American Psychiatric Association (APA) removed homosexuality as a mental illness from its diagnostic manual. The depiction of queer people as outlaws radicalized against the norms of society in queer cinema and slashers of the time amplify the very real conditions of institutional discrimination. I am routinely reminded of the striking image of Dr. John E. Fryer, a gay psychiatrist who presented at the 1972 APA Annual Meeting in an appeal for compassion toward gay patients and colleagues. Out of fear for his career and continued participation in a heteronormative professional society, he did so only under the condition that his identity be hidden. So, he sat there at the American Psychiatric Association as a qualified psychiatrist under the pseudonym Dr. Henry Anonymous, wearing a rubber mask and a wig of curly black hair.[19] I always compare this visual likeness to the screen image of Leatherface released one year later. Though this is surely a coincidence, the metaphorical image of queer people as masked figures emerging from the shadows to confront society pervades queer history.

The practice of mask wearing can also be seen prominently in the language of the 1950s homophile movement. Early gay rights organization Mattachine Society took its name from the medieval European political theater of the Feast of Fools, in which an unmarried fraternity of masked performers would perform

dances that staged the triumph of the oppressed over the church
and state through the intervention of a fool. Cofounder Harry
Hay argued that the public service of the masked performers in
exposing and critiquing oppression during the Feast of Fools mirrored the potential for Mattachine Society.[20] Likewise, we see the
theme of masks as a metaphor for the burden of secrecy throughout homophile literature. The April 1958 cover story in *Mattachine
Review* by Bob Bishop espoused the political and personal ben-
efits of gays and lesbians coming out under the title "Discard the
Mask."[21] Gay periodical *ONE Magazine*'s February 1959 cover
touted "The Tragedy of Masks," referencing a poem therein by
Doyle Eugene Livingston that likens queer life to lonely actors
performing in masks.[22] October 1957's cover for Lesbian magazine *The Ladder* featured a drawing of a figure holding a mask
with one tear beneath the eye. Inside, a poem titled "Disguise" by
Audrey Kern opens with the lines "A mask I wear / For the world
to see."[23] Though the masked slashers common in the 1970s have
no intrinsic historical connection with early literature in the gay
rights movement, the premise of a masked character emerging
as an anarchic political agitator does resonate with themes that
I have spelled out thus far in both queer cinema and slashers.
Figures such as Divine and Leatherface, faces obscured by clay
and rubber, wreaking havoc, and seeking the murderous demise
of "normal" society. I hope this history clarifies how the image of
a masked outsider who terrorizes the ruling class and stages their
overthrow might be understood as having a queer political function. Especially given the role of the fool, or masked performer,
in conceptualizing early gay activism and the dominant allegory
of being masked as a part of a historical queer self-understanding.

Another important intersection between queer cinema and
horror can be seen through preslasher films that utilize queer talent both in front of and behind the camera. I would like to highlight some horror films by queer filmmakers that further engage
with toxic representations of the church, the nuclear family, and

Christmas. The first is gay director Andy Milligan's *Seeds* (1968). Milligan was a filmmaker working under restricted financial circumstances who often called on nontraditional actors and friends for parts. His films were sometimes marketed as horror and other times as sexploitation, but more practically he was making deeply sincere queer melodramas about broken families and legacies of sexual abuse. He is unique as a figure whose work amalgamates underground queer cinema and commercial grindhouse fare.[24] *Seeds* introduces us to the dysfunctional Manning family, led by demoralizing matriarch Claris (Maggie Rogers), who is angered to learn her daughter Carol (Candy Hammond) has invited the family home for Christmas because Claris, in her own words, "hates them." As the evening progresses, family secrets reemerge, including a past incestuous relationship between Carol and her brother Michael (Anthony Moscini) and the child sexual abuse of their younger brother Buster (Gene Connolly) by his older brother Matthew (Neil Flanagan), who is now a priest. Buster is the most sensitive character of the film, and we are made to feel for him as his mother embarrasses him with a list of the behavioral grievances that have gotten him thrown out of every school he's ever attended, including queer sexual relations with other boys. As the family breaks down into devious double-crossings and lurid sexual encounters, an unseen murderer begins killing them one by one. During a histrionic confrontation between Buster and Claris, she remarks that her children are all "bad seeds," to which he returns, "A bad seed comes from a diseased plant," which feels tantamount to the film's thesis on family relations.

Gay filmmaker Curtis Harrington began his career making pioneering experimental queer short films such as *Fragment of Seeking* (1946) and is credited, along with collaborator Kenneth Anger, for beginning a crucial movement of post–World War II gay underground avant-garde cinema.[25] His work slowly progressed toward feature-length projects that blended his atmospheric style with horror narratives, beginning with 1961's eerie mermaid romance *Night Tide*. In 1971, the Harrington horror film *What's the Matter with Helen?*, starring Hollywood legends Debbie Reynolds and Shelley Winters was released. The film tells the story of two women seeking a new beginning after their sons are convicted of murder: Adelle (Reynolds), a would-be Hollywood star with a Jean Harlow hairdo, and Helen (Winters), a repressed churchgoing lesbian who obviously loves Adelle and then tragically kills her.[26] However, in Harrington's film, the motive to kill is not innately due to Helen's queerness but instead due to her tortured life of church-endorsed self-loathing and denial. In his autobiography, Harrington described it as "my portrait of the destructive narrow-mindedness of Christian fundamentalism, as exemplified by the character of Helen, whose hypocritical inability to face the truth of her sexuality brings only tragedy to those around her and madness to herself."[27]

Harrington and Winters reunited for another film released that same year, *Whoever Slew Auntie Roo?*, in which Winters stars as the self-professed Aunt Roo, a seemingly cheerful and generous woman with a secret. Each year she invites a selection of children from a local orphanage to spend Christmas at her luxurious home. However, she is still grieving the tragic death of her young daughter, and on this Christmas, she's selected young Katy (Chloe Franks) to kidnap as a replacement. In one scene, Roo reads "'Twas the Night Before Christmas" to a room full of eager children and then lapses into a remorseful monologue about her choice to leave her career in the theater "for love" that concludes with a creepy thousand-yard stare as she tells the small children that she still talks to her deceased husband, who has only gone to "the other side of the mirror." The film recalls the macabre fable Hansel and Gretel, juxtaposing picturesque Christmas scenes with the undercurrent of danger in accepting toys and sweets from Roo. The film's finale features a delusional Aunt Roo brandishing a meat cleaver and squaring off with Katy's brother Christopher (Mark Lester) as he attempts to rescue his sister. In the end, Christopher traps Roo in a fire that burns her alive, mirroring the ending of Hansel and Gretel, wherein Gretel pushes the witch into her own oven.

Several of the threads discussed throughout this chapter—a critique of the nuclear family, the metamorphizing of Christmas into a site of trauma, the radical politics of gay liberation, and the crossover in talent between queer and slasher cinema of the 1960s and '70s—come together in Theodore Gershuny's *Silent Night, Bloody Night*, shot in 1970 and first released in 1972 as *Night of the Dark Full Moon* before being rereleased in 1973 under its more popular Christmas-themed title.[28] Director Gershuny cast his then wife, Mary Woronov, as the film's lead, Diane. Woronov was a figure in the New York countercultural art scene, notably performing as a whip dancer with The Velvet Underground and appearing in Andy Warhol films such as *Chelsea Girls* (1966).[29] The Warhol Factory and its many superstars feature in the film's dramatization of queer rebellion. It opens with voiceover narration by Diane explaining the 1950 Christmas Eve death of Wilfred Butler (Phillip Bruns), accompanied by the image of a man running aflame across the clean white snow. The film then cuts to a family photo of the Butlers in nostalgic sepia with the isolated voice of a small child singing "Silent Night" on the soundtrack before transitioning to the provocative title card: *Silent Night, Bloody Night* (with "bloody" in red font). Twenty years later, Wilfred's grandson Jeffrey (James Patterson) has listed the family home for sale despite the request in Butler's will that it remain "standing untouched to remind the world of its inhumanity and cruelty." According to the voiceover, this news triggers the violent escape of an unknown figure from a psychiatric hospital. The escape is filmed using first-person camera, and the subsequent lurking of the figure around the Butler house is routinely shot using first-person POV until the time of the final revelation, a detail that interestingly situates this stylistically in conversation with later slashers. The mysterious figure, whose

POV we occupy, is shown murdering various townspeople on Christmas Eve in settings populated with Christmas decorations and scored to Christmas songs. The tonal counterpoint between murder and festive Christmas fare functions similarly to how I have described in other Christmas slashers. In one particularly morbid indictment of religious convictions, the killer murders the lawyer facilitating the sale of the home (Patrick O'Neal) and his lover (Astrid Heeren) during sex and then places a crucifix inside the lawyer's bloody palm.

Throughout the film, the leaders of the small town receive mysterious phone calls from someone identifying themselves as "Marianne," who tries to lure them back to the Butler residence. This includes Diane's father, the mayor (Walter Abel), the sheriff (Walter Klavun), the newspaper publisher (John Carridine), and the communications director who operates the telephone switchboard (Fran Stevens). In the film's conclusion, we learn through voiceover that Wilfred Butler is alive and faked his own death by setting a random squatter on fire. The real Wilfred is the mysterious creeping killer we saw escape from the psychiatric hospital at the start of the film. He has returned to seek vengeance on the town's leaders and called them to his old home using Marianne, the name of his deceased daughter whose death he blames on them. Many years prior, following the death of Butler's wife, he raped and impregnated his fifteen-year-old daughter, Marianne, who gave birth to their son, Jeffrey. Butler subsequently turned his home into some form of barbaric psychiatric facility to which Marianne was admitted following her traumatic assault and pregnancy. When Butler was dissatisfied with Marianne's so-called treatment, he vengefully released those trapped at the facility (credited in the film as inmates) knowing they would overtake the ruling class of abusive doctors and professionals who have treated them poorly. A Christmas party shown on grainy sepia film depicts the facility's staff dancing and celebrating while feasting on an extravagant dinner and getting drunk on Butler's booze. They're framed as wealthy lushes who extract their income and power from the oppression of a marginalized community marked by difference. The inmates are played by the superstars of the Warhol Factory, including Ondine, Jack Smith, and Tally Brown—underground, countercultural, and queer artists.[30] We additionally learn that the entire town as we know it, including the mayor, sheriff, newspaper publisher, and communications director, were all formerly among these inmates. In essence, *Silent Night, Bloody Night* portrays an oppressed class of queer others radically overthrowing their captors and making a new society for themselves, becoming their own leaders, and taking charge of the institutional powers that gay liberation sought to reimagine: the media, the law, the government. *Silent Night, Bloody Night* imagines a social uprising for the marginalized and uses queer figures of its countercultural moment in revolutionary roles. It notably bridges queer cinema of the period with the still-emerging tropes that would go on to become quintessential to the slasher. It, along with the rest of the films in this chapter, point toward an interesting overlap, demonstrating that queer cinema and slasher cinema may have more enmeshed stylistic, thematic, and production histories than previously thought.

The overlap between queer independent cinema and horror cinema of the 1970s also speaks to the ongoing theme of universalizing and minoritizing queer discourses discussed in the introduction of this book. Alexander Doty and Harry Benshoff note the ability of horror to position all spectators—straight and queer—in a universalized queer position. Albeit, for most straight audiences, only temporarily. However, explicitly queer films from distinctly queer production contexts with queer casts and crews have been treated as niche objects of perversion. While slashers may inflame moralistic audiences (a quality that, I argue, gives them queer appeal), they are not marginalized as "queer films" and as such maintain wider appeal for mainstream heterosexual audiences. It is important to remain mindful that although

I argue in this chapter that queer cinema and horror cinema of the 1960s and '70s meaningfully overlap, they are not perceived in the same ways. Curtis Harrington's career provides one example of this as his '60s mainstream horror movies with Shelley Winters were able to speak to a more universalized audience and were therefore far more widely circulated than his '40s avant-garde queer shorts. But only, of course, if Shelley Winters's sapphic love for Debbie Reynolds was played as subtext, imbued by the director and actor but never spoken aloud. Mainstream horror can *feel* queer, can be made *by* queers, but queer avant-garde films made by queer filmmakers for majority queer audiences were legally policed in the '60s as obscene. In 1964, around the same time Curtis Harrington's sideshow horror movie *Night Tide* was making its theatrical premiere, his former collaborator Kenneth Anger's experimental queer short *Scorpio Rising* (1963), a homoerotic pop musical full of Brando-ish bikers, was the subject of an obscenity trial. The Cinema Theater was raided by the Los Angeles vice squad, copies of the film were confiscated, and its programmer Mike Getz was arrested for showing "an obscene movie."[31] Jonas Mekas, film critic for *The Village Voice*, and three others were also arrested during a 1964 screening of Jack Smith's queer film *Flaming Creatures* (1963) at New Bowery Theater in New York and charged with showing an obscene film (Mekas allegedly provided the print, which was seized by police).[32] Almost one decade later, the film's director, Jack Smith, appeared as an inmate resisting abusive imprisonment in the Christmas slasher *Silent Night, Bloody Night* (1972). While horror's universal queer appeal has an important function, it does not resolve the minoritizing blame and tangible discrimination against cinematic works depicting queer lives from queer perspectives. The remaining chapters of this book transition to discuss queer slashers made by queer filmmakers that more directly speak for and about queer experiences, beginning with queer auteur John Waters, whose theories about queer aesthetics have influenced much of this book.

NOTES

1. As a historical note, it's worth mentioning here that we should be mindful that these formations are relatively new, as *Black Christmas* and other films of the early to mid-1970s are commonly seen as early slashers or precursors to the slasher. So, here I am suggesting this scene demonstrates something in its early stages rather than points out something already common, as it is not yet so.

2. Gay Liberation Front, "Manifesto," published 1971, revised 1978, reprinted by Fordham University Internet History Sourcebooks Project, https://sourcebooks.fordham.edu/pwh/glf-london.asp.

3. Eve Kosofsky Sedgwick, *Tendencies* (Durham, NC: Duke University Press, 1993), 5.

4. Sedgwick, *Tendencies*, 8.

5. John Waters, *Crackpot: The Obsessions of John Waters* (New York: Macmillan, 1986), 116–17.

6. Waters, *Crackpot*, 119–20.

7. Melissa Locker, "A Christmas Conversation with John Waters," *TIME*, December 10, 2013, http://entertainment.time.com/2013/12/10/a-christmas-conversation-with-john-waters.

8. *Silent Night, Evil Night* is the original US release title of Bob Clark's *Black Christmas* (1974).

9. Lewis Jackson and John Waters, "Commentaries," *Christmas Evil*, Blu-ray and DVD, directed by Lewis Jackson (Bridgeport, CT: Vinegar Syndrome, 2014).

10. *At the Movies*, season 3, episode 9, "Stop Making Sense/Falling in Love/Paris Texas," featuring Gene Siskel and Roger Ebert, aired November 24, 1984, in broadcast syndication. Barmark's sexuality is discussed by friend Howard Ronsenman in "Why Being Gay in the '70s in New York and L.A. Was Magic—and How Hollywood Has Changed," *Hollywood Reporter*, May 3, 2019, https://www.hollywoodreporter.com/news/general-news/why-being-gay-70s-new-york-la-was-magic-guest-column-1205565.

11. "'Killer Santa' Movie Protested," *Washington Post*, November 15, 1984, D15.

12. "Poor Earnings Curtail Christmas Horror Film," *New York Times*, November 24, 1984, 11.

13. "Parents Yell as Santa Pulls a Slay," *Philadelphia Daily News*, November 10, 1984, 9.

14. A similar scene can also be found in *Tales from the Crypt* (Freddie Francis, 1972), in which a mother played by Joan Collins hides from a killer in a Santa costume only to learn her daughter has let him in the house, gleeful that Santa has finally arrived.

15. A more direct homage is also seen in *Pink Flamingos*, where Divine walks the streets of Baltimore to the same Little Richard song.

16. The image recalls Waters's own anecdote about his grandmother being pinned under a tree.

17. Robin Wood, "The American Family Comedy: From *Meet Me in St. Louis* to *The Texas Chainsaw Massacre*," in *Robin Wood on the Horror Film: Collected Essays and Reviews*, ed. Barry Keith Grant (Detroit: Wayne State University Press, 2018), 179.

18. For a history of state decriminalization and the Supreme Court rulings on antisodomy laws, see Richard Weinmeyer, "The Decriminalization of Sodomy in the United States," *American Medical Association Journal of Ethics* 16, no. 11 (November 2014): 916–22.

19. For images and context, see Ellen Barry, "He Spurred a Revolution in Psychiatry. Then He 'Disappeared,'" *New York Times*, May 2, 2022, https://www.nytimes.com/2022/05/02/health/john-fryer-psychiatry.html.

20. Harry Hay, *Radically Gay: Gay Liberation in the Words of Its Founder* (Boston, MA: Beacon, 1996), 110–15.

21. Bob Bishop, "Discard the Mask," *Mattachine Review* 4, no. 4 (April 1958): 14–16, 21–24.

22. Doyle Eugene Livingston, "The Tragedy of Masks," *ONE Magazine* 7, no. 2 (February 1959): 6–7.

23. Audrey Kern, "Disguise," *The Ladder* 2, no. 1 (October 1957): 13.

24. For discussions of Milligan in the context of both queer underground cinema and commercial grindhouse cinema, see Rob Craig, *Gutter Auteur: The Films of Andy Milligan* (Jefferson, NC: McFarland, 2013).

25. Jack Stevenson, "From the Bedroom to the Bijou: A Secret History of Gay American Sex Cinema," *Film Quarterly* 51, no. 1 (fall 1997): 26.

26. Winters discusses her choice to play the role as a lesbian in Jessie Lilley, "Chilling Winters: Shelley Winters Talks About *What's the Matter with Helen?*," *Scarlet Street* no. 11 (summer 1993): 65–67.

27. Curtis Harrington, *Nice Guys Don't Work in Hollywood: The Adventures of an Aesthete in the Movie Business* (Chicago: Drag City, 2013). Kindle edition.

28. "AFI Catalog of Feature Films: *Silent Night, Bloody Night*," https://catalog.afi.com/Catalog/moviedetails/54239.

29. For details, see Mary Woronov, *WARHOL Told by WORONOV—Swimming Underground: My Time at Andy Warhol's Factory* (Los Angeles: Montaldo, 2013).

30. Uniquely, actress and trans icon Candy Darling, though a star from the Warhol Factory, portrays a party guest of the doctors, not an inmate, likely because of the mainstream glamour aesthetic she exhibited.

31. Mike Getz, interview by Alison Kozberg, *Alternative Projections*, June 12, 2010, https://www.alternativeprojections.com/oral-histories/mike-getz/.

32. "Avant-Garde Movie Seized as Obscene," *New York Times*, March 4, 1964, 33.

THREE

—ππ—

THE SUN WILL COME OUT
TOMORROW, OR WILL IT?

IT DOESN'T SEEM LIKE A particularly controversial statement. That the sun will come out tomorrow. However, it does presume a certain continuity in experience. That the sun will rise, as it has before, and that the speaker of the song will be around to see it.

John Waters's 1994 slasher comedy *Serial Mom* hinges on a crucial deployment of this popular song: "Tomorrow" from the Broadway musical *Annie* and its 1982 movie adaptation, directed by John Huston.[1] *Serial Mom* tells a fictive tale about serial killer and suburban housewife Beverly Sutphin (Kathleen Turner) but uses the stylistic trappings of docudrama or true crime. Opening titles note how "names have been changed," and reoccurring date and time titles appear as visual gags throughout the film to suggest a faux verisimilitude.[2] Beverly is introduced to us as a loving mother and spouse, a peachy-keen neighbor, and an upstanding citizen of the affluent white suburbs of Baltimore.[3] However, we quickly learn that Beverly has secrets. She executes those she feels are guilty of moral infractions against the quality of living among the picturesque suburban community in which she resides. These include small gripes, like stealing a parking spot, chewing gum, or wearing white after Labor Day. Beverly's executions are methodical and targeted. She kills the people she feels have done wrong according to her own set of values. She is not presented as having memory lapses or being out of control, characteristics we see in films such as William Castle's *Strait-Jacket* (1964), in which an ax-wielding Joan Crawford is unsure if she has committed murders after returning home from a psychiatric hospital (Waters features a clip from this film on a TV screen during *Serial Mom*).

In a climactic scene of murder, Beverly follows Mrs. Jensen (Patsy Grady Abrams) home from the local video store after learning that she routinely does not rewind her VHS rentals. Mrs. Jensen pops in her latest movie of choice: *Annie* (John Huston, 1982).[4] She sits back in her reclining chair, sticks out her bare toes, and implores her dog to lick them. Beside her sits a sandwich, which she happily takes a bite from as the credits roll. The opening titles feature images of the actors placed inside the frame of Annie's locket, an important prop to the plot of the film, while the voice of Annie (Aileen Quinn) sings with gusto the most well-known song of the musical: "Tomorrow." Meanwhile, Beverly breaks the glass window of the kitchen door and reaches in to unlock it. She warmly greets and pets Mrs. Jensen's dog and takes the knife Mrs. Jensen used to slice her lunch meat from the kitchen table. She enters the living room where Mrs. Jensen loudly sings along with the refrain of "Tomorrow." Raising the knife, ready for the kill, Beverly reconsiders and appears to give up as she returns to the kitchen. However, she instead picks up the leg of lamb from which Mrs. Jensen cut the meat for her sandwich. Satisfied in her choice, Beverly once again approaches a clueless, singing Mrs. Jensen, and as the music blares "Tomorrow!"—Beverly smashes the leg of lamb against Mrs. Jensen's skull—*thwap*—and the two accompany each other in a dance of point-counterpoint—"Tomorrow!" *thwap* "Tomorrow!" *thwap*—as Mrs. Jensen is violently murdered. The camera looks up at Beverly from a low angle, taking on a similar position to the victim cowering beneath her as Beverly lowers the final blows. Beverly is now singing along with each crash of the meat slab: "You're only a" *thwap* "day" *thwap*

Fig 3.1 Beverly brandishing a lethal leg of lamb in *Serial Mom* (1994) while an unsuspecting Mrs. Jensen sings along to "Tomorrow," unaware she's about to eat it.

"a" *thwap* "way!" A shot of the TV reveals little Aileen Quinn's picture as Annie set inside a heart-shaped locket with blood and gore splattered across the screen. The camera cuts to Beverly's angered face standing over the body as she shouts, "Rewind!" Then we pan from a shot of Mrs. Jensen lying dead on the floor to the bloody TV as static bars fill the screen and the credits sequence rewinds, recoiling back to its starting position. On her way out, we see that Beverly has fed the remaining leg of lamb to the dog to do away with any evidence.[5]

Much of this chapter will be spent trying to unpack why this scene feels particularly seismic in impact and wit to me. It is catalyzed by an affective intensity underlying my own repeated viewings of the scene and my experiences showing it to students and colleagues. I feel that it always evokes an amorphous, indescribable reverberation of energy. Something I can't quite phrase. It puts cinematic language together in a manner that captures a feeling I'd like for this book to try to articulate at the level of conscious thought. Even if it fails. I hope to use this queer-directed

THE SUN WILL COME OUT TOMORROW, OR WILL IT?   99

slasher as the impetus for explaining the need I have to pivot the book here from an account of queer resonance in slashers writ large to a study of how queer filmmakers have and continue to reforge the queer meanings of the slasher. To begin, I explore how the scene works within the film. I explain how *Serial Mom* positions itself in the company of slashers and as a reaction to them. Then I contextualize the scene in terms of both queer history and queer theory to explain the particularly powerful experience it offers and to characterize my project moving forward with regard to queer artists reimagining canonical slashers.

This scene plays on the ironic contrast between the apparent message of the song "Tomorrow" (an optimistic look toward a happier future) and the arrival, as counterpoint, of Beverly Sutphin, who comically refutes the thesis of the song to which Mrs. Jensen sings along by brutally murdering her. Of course, this means Mrs. Jensen will not, in fact, see tomorrow as the song had promised. There is also a tonal contrast here: the chipper, cheerful "Tomorrow" and the opening credits of *Annie* mixed with the grim and brutally realistic blood-splattered murder. That central contrast is colored further with comic details like the leg of lamb and the fake-out of returning to the kitchen. Even the act of murder has within itself a meld of feeling both funny and brutal. The leg of lamb signals a humorous flourish, but it does not undo or undermine that the murder is uncomfortable to watch. We're also left with uncertainty over how to feel about the motivation for Beverly's violence: is it funny to kill over "be kind, rewind," or is it just an added component of tragedy? Can it be and feel like both? To address some of the dissonance here, I'd like to recall the scene from *Black Christmas* (Bob Clark, 1974) discussed at the start of chapter 2. In that scene, the seemingly innocent faces of children singing Christmas carols are crosscut with a violent stabbing. I argued that this crosscutting effectively created new connections between traditional Christmas imagery and experiences of trauma, and that by opening up Christmas media to these traumatic associations, the holiday expanded to include new and different feelings, effectively queering Christmas. The scene in *Serial Mom* varies this contrast by allowing for humor to pervade both in the "Tomorrow" portions of the scene and in the moments of murder. It's varied by the fact that the murder and the song occur in the same physical space, and the singer of the song is now the victim of the murder, disavowing the distance created by keeping the events in separate shots connected only through editing. Unlike with *Black Christmas*, Beverly acknowledges and participates in the musical moment during her murder by finishing the final lines to Mrs. Jensen's song. The scene in *Black Christmas* points to how crosscut images allow for new and unexpected connections, acknowledging that images of murder, or anything really, could be crosscut with Christmas caroling to create new associations with Christmas imagery. However, the scene in *Serial Mom* transforms this pattern by moving from contrast toward complete integration. We experience the beginning of Beverly's attack as irony, the rebuttal to the wide-eyed optimism that there will be a tomorrow. However, as the camera lingers on Beverly's brutality and she begins to sing along, the scene asserts surprisingly that Beverly's worldview is not antithetical but congruous with the spirit of "Tomorrow." She is not repelled or off-put by the song, doesn't cringe or mock it. She finishes it with gusto, and that crescendo of the song is equal to the crescendo of her violence. To Beverly, her act of murder is what will bring about that happier tomorrow.

An important shift in *Serial Mom* relative to many classical slashers is that the killer here is not an outsider, someone who encroaches on the desired safety and security of white heteronormative bourgeois suburban communities. The killer, Beverly, is a community member rooted within the suburbs themselves.[6] She is not seemingly marked by queer traits of gender and/or sexual difference, but rather she presents as hyper-normative and conformist. We meet her serving cereal (a pun on the film's title) to her family with the joyful obedience of a 1950s TV sitcom mom. She carries on breakfast table conversation, making small corrections about politeness ("Don't say 'hate,' dear. 'Hate' is a very serious word") as she cautiously eyes a fly that's ruining her picture-perfect family image by flitting around and perching on toast. She smiles with glee after she locates and executes the fly with her fly swatter. It's the first scene demonstrating Beverly's compulsive need to correct what she perceives as errors to her vision of heteronormative suburban bliss. As Waters puts it, "Serial mom looks at murder as a household cleaning problem."[7] In chapter 1, I argued that the killer's attacks in the slasher commonly take the form of resisting normativity through abrasive assaults on stereotypical teen archetypes, such as jocks and prom queens, and heteronormative adolescent rituals, such as graduation and summer camp. In chapter 2, I suggest likewise that an affront to the traditional meanings of Christmas similarly created queer resonances for the slasher. What stands out to me here is that Beverly's violence does not resist or disenchant such scenes of the heteronormative suburban nuclear family but instead seems designed to carefully protect and preserve this ideal, rooting out intrusions where she must. The opening scene presents us with something of a literal "fly in the ointment" that upsets the perfection of Beverly's catalog-worthy tableau, and she makes the choice to terminate that problem.

Beverly continues to similarly terminate anyone she feels is disrupting the normative perfection of her suburban family life, including her son Chip's (Matthew Lillard) high school math teacher, Mr. Stubbins (John Badila). During a parent-teacher conference, Stubbins observes that Chip is doing excellently in school, but he has concerns about Chip's "sick" interest in horror films, brandishing a gore-filled drawing Chip made in class inspired by *Blood Feast* (Herschell Gordon Lewis, 1963). Stubbins probes Beverly about problems at home, inquiring about parental divorce or alcoholism as a reason for the behavior. He even goes as far as asking Beverly if Chip ever tortured animals, suggesting the early signs of Chip being a serial killer. After Beverly assures Stubbins no such problem exists, he chides her with, "Well, you're doing something wrong, Mrs. Sutphin." Stubbins's call to pathologize Chip's violent drawing recalls a scene from *Silent Night, Deadly Night* (Charles E. Sellier, Jr., 1982), discussed in chapter 2, in which the burgeoning serial killer Billy is scolded after he draws a bloody Christmas scene that reflects his parents' violent murders by a killer Santa. However, *Serial Mom* makes a pointed shift here by deliberately not pathologizing Chip's interests in horror or gore. In fact, the film plays consistently on the irony that "upstanding" authority figures within the suburban community deliberately overlook actual serial killer Beverly because she conforms to normative standards. Waters chose to shoot Beverly's murder of Mr. Stubbins at Towson High School, where friend and collaborator Divine was once a student, citing the pleasure he took in shooting the murder of a teacher on the school's premises. "I wanted to film killing a teacher there because Divine left the school. Every day they beat him up. The teachers were mean to him. He was traumatized daily in this actual school."[8] The choice was a deliberate retort to the acts of queer bashing that haunt the school's halls. *Serial Mom* repeatedly stages scenes in which authority figures target harmless characters with fringe interests deemed taboo or repellant. When Beverly runs over Mr. Stubbins violently with her car (then backs over him to seal the deal), the only witness is local stoner Luann Hodges (Kim Swann) who confirms the color and model of Beverly's car. However, Beverly and her family quickly laugh off the witness as a "pothead" when watching TV news later that evening.

A similar interaction occurs at a flea market when Beverly follows Carl (Lonnie Horsey), the rude and unfaithful boyfriend of her daughter Misty (Ricki Lake), into a men's public bathroom with a fire poker and murders him. Prior to the attack, we see Marvin Pickles (Tim Caggiano) cruising for gay oral sex at a glory hole inside one of the bathroom stalls. Peeking through the hole to check for a willing partner, he is shocked instead to see Beverly clutching her fire poker. He flees for his safety. Following her murder of Carl, we see Beverly carrying on with sales at the flea market, undisturbed. Meanwhile, Marvin is being interrogated and frisked. We hear a snippet of dialogue in which he insists to police that there was a woman in the men's room, but he is clearly being ignored and targeted as a suspect in the crime. Immediately following this scene, Beverly is shown selling a Pee-wee Herman doll at the flea market for a high price. In a DVD commentary recorded in 1999, Waters remarks on the doll's inclusion, saying, "I wanted to show, sort of, support to him when all that ridiculous stuff happened to him." He is referring here to the 1991 arrest of actor Paul Reubens by an undercover police officer for masturbating at a pornographic movie theater in Sarasota, Florida.[9] The incident made Reubens the target of public mockery and disdain. CBS pulled upcoming reruns of *Pee-wee's Playhouse* (1986–90), and toy retailer Toys"R"Us removed Pee-wee Herman dolls, like the one Beverly sells in the film, from shelves.[10] The gesture amplifies the film's observations about police punitively harassing sexuality and cruising rather than focusing on the physical harm and violence of those aligned with heteronormative bourgeois values. Horror gore hounds, recreational cannabis users, and men cruising for gay sex are not pathologized by Waters's film. They are shown as unjust targets for community disdain and scapegoats for community problems. Most importantly, these characters are not killers. While they may express some friction with the normative standards set by the community, they pose no real threat. It is Beverly who does the film's killing to preserve the normative facade.

Over the course of the film, Beverly's internal life is shown to be hypocritically at odds with the facade she presents. When detectives inquire with the Sutphins about obscene phone calls and mail threats sent to their neighbor Dottie Hinkle (Mink Stole),

Beverly playacts shock and contempt for the idea. They reveal to
her a piece of mail that spells out in cut and pasted ransom note
letters "I'll get you pussy face," to which she replies, "I've never
even said the p-word out loud." In their car afterward, the detectives liken Beverly to "Beaver Cleaver's mother," referring to the
popular and archetypal family sitcom *Leave It to Beaver* (1957–63).
One concludes, "Mrs. Sutphin's about as normal and nice a lady
as we're ever going to find." The film cuts immediately following
this line to Beverly dialing her phone with a grin on her face.
A split screen shows us the recipient of the call: Dottie. Dottie
answers, and a gleeful Beverly asks, "Is this the cocksucker residence?" Mrs. Cleaver she is not. Beverly's behavior of harassing
Dottie with sexual phone calls evokes the history in the slasher
of women receiving scary phone calls from killers, often sexual
in nature or with heavy breathing. In chapter 2, I discussed how
in *Black Christmas*, Jess (Olivia Hussey) is working with police
to try to track a mysterious caller whom the sorority house nick-
names "the moaner." During the first call shown in the film, he
makes harassing sexual remarks, stating, "Suck my juicy cock."
What seems particularly novel about Beverly's call relative to
this one, though, is that she is not portrayed as taking sexual
gratification from the call. Her interest is more cunning and sinister. She smiles and suppresses laughter throughout. She wants
to punish Dottie. We see in a flashback that Dottie cut Beverly
off in her car and stole a parking spot, which appears to be what
marked her as one of Beverly's targets. In a later scene following
the murder of Mr. Stubbins, Beverly interrupts Chip's screening
of *Blood Feast* and asks his friends to leave. She repeats Mr. Stubbins's concerns about Chip's interest in horror movies being bad
for him. Then she lifts a swimsuit magazine by the corner with
two fingers as if it were too filthy to touch and pointedly returns
it to Chip's friend Scotty (Justin Whalin), making it known she
does not approve of his sexual interests. The film signals that her
prudishness about sex and horror is ultimately just about public

appearances, as once everyone has gone, we see her swiftly get into bed and ask Chip to replay the bloody scene they had been watching. At night, Beverly is shown reading books on ornithology while speaking with her husband, Eugene (Sam Waterson), but the camera reveals that inside her book she is caressing photos of Charles Manson. When Eugene later searches their bedroom, he finds bodybuilding photos of Richard Speck and voicemails from Ted Bundy addressing Beverly by name. Beverly's secret vulgarity and interest in serial killers reveal that the obsessively manicured facade she kills to protect is only about public perception. Privately, she is not averse to sex or violence. However, she has calibrated these private interests in such a way that they operate in service of the public image she wants to maintain for herself and her family. One in which chewing gum is taboo but violent murder is acceptable if it preserves her image.

Beverly is the inverse of Chip and his friend Birdie (Patricia Dunnock), with whom he shares a love for horror movies, as they are horror fans whose stomachs turn at actual violence. Birdie is immediately intrigued by Beverly when her murders are discovered. She conflates the idea of having a town killer with the idea of being in a horror movie, telling Beverly, "You're bigger than Freddy or Jason, only you're a real person!" But when Birdie sees the body of Beverly's victim, she bursts into anguished tears, realizing that her love of horror movies is nothing like violence in real life. Despite his description of a childhood fascination with playing "car crash" and his extolling the virtues of violent imagery in "Why I Love Violence," Waters plainly asserts, "I hate real violence . . . but I can watch Herschell Gordon Lewis gore movies for two hours. Everybody knows the difference between real violence and fake violence."[11] *Serial Mom* echoes this dichotomy by drawing a sharp contrast between Beverly's actual violence and the fun of representational gore. It also develops the idea that Beverly's public-facing normativity conceals secrets that are dangerous and cause harm whereas the openly horror-obsessed Chip and Birdie pose no threat. As is also the case with the openly sexual bathroom cruiser at the flea market and the self-assured high school stoner who witnessed Beverly's murder of Mr. Stubbins. Their honesty around horror, sex, or drugs make them targets of suspicion. However, these suspicions overlook the true threat to the community's safety: ultra-normative Beverly Sutphin.

To contextualize Beverly as an archetype within a broader queer history, I want to consider her in relation to the famously antigay singer Anita Bryant, who cultivated a traditionally wholesome public image. She was second runner-up in the 1959 Miss America pageant and performed as part of the halftime show at Super Bowl V in 1971. Her music career included a mix of secular hits like "Paper Roses" and religious hymns. In the 1970s, she became well known as a spokesperson for Florida orange juice. In a popular advertisement, Bryant is seen waking her children for breakfast and serving them orange juice while conveying the upbeat slogan "Breakfast without orange juice is like a day without sunshine." The tableau of a cheerful white suburban mother serving children breakfast is not unlike the opening moments of *Serial Mom*, in which the Sutphin family sits around the table while Beverly happily serves them cereal. Upon the film's release, critics picked up on the connection between Beverly and US media tropes about TV moms. Soren Anderson of *The News Tribune* stated, "Get your mind around: Donna Reed, chasing some poor teenager around the neighborhood with a butcher knife," likening Beverly to the famous TV mom of *The Donna Reed Show* (1958–66).[12] Other critics reference June Cleaver, Harriet Nelson, Carol Brady, etc.[13] They point to the way that Beverly is seen as one in a lineage of idyllic mom types rather than a freestanding or completely original character to be understood without reference. As with Vera Dika's assertion that the teens murdered in slashers are so nondescript as to be "of the television commercial,"[14] Beverly's characterization gives us the distinct impression we should see her as a commercial image, a mom from TV serving breakfast or selling orange juice. While Bryant was not the star of a sitcom, she arguably participated in this mediated tradition of the idyllic mom archetype as she was quite literally a mom "of the television commercial." Like Beverly, Bryant's hyper-normative image housed darker ambitions. Namely, she would go on to become the face of homophobia in the 1970s. Waters himself has commented on Bryant's legacy as one of mixed blessings. In an interview with *The Advocate*, he noted that Bryant galvanized queer communities into political action. However, he also likened her to the more contemporary figure Kim Davis, the Kentucky clerk who refused to issue same-sex marriage licenses after the 2015 US Supreme Court ruling upholding marriage equality. Waters remarked, "Well, we got a new villain!"[15] His comment implies that Waters views Bryant as a gay villain, an emblem of the movement working against us who simultaneously galvanizes the complacent among us to take notice of queer issues.

Bryant's public role in antigay politics began in 1977, when she joined a campaign against a civil rights ordinance in Dade County, Florida, intended to protect homosexuals from discrimination in areas such as housing and employment. After the ordinance was passed, conversative and religious groups formed an oppositional organization called Save Our Children that hoped to collect enough signatures to force a referendum. Bryant's fame made her a highly visible spokesperson for the antigay cause. She used her position to stoke fear in parents that homosexuals were dangerous pedophiles whose employment as schoolteachers would put their children at risk. At the 1977 hearing on the referendum, Bryant opened her remarks by insisting she had "no prejudice" and cited her experience in the entertainment industry working with homosexuals as evidence she was not a bigot. She went on to frame her request as a civil rights issue for herself and her children, blending motherhood and religion together in her remarks. She stated, "God created us so our children would be dependent upon us as their parents for their lives. And I, for one, will do everything I can as a citizen, as a Christian, and especially as a mother to insure [*sic*] that they have the right to a healthy and morally good life."[16] In her memoir published that same year, *The Anita Bryant Story*, she echoed a prominent homophobic refrain insinuating homosexuals will "recruit" or pervert children, stating, "Homosexuals cannot reproduce—so they must recruit. And to freshen their ranks, they must recruit the youth of America."[17] An ad paid for by Save Our Children encouraging viewers to vote for repeal of the ordinance outrightly asserted that homosexuals put children at risk of sexual abuse. It juxtaposed footage of families watching a marching band at the Florida Orange Bowl Parade with footage of men in drag and leather gear from San Francisco's Pride Parade. The accompanying voiceover: "The Orange Bowl Parade—Miami's gift to the nation. Wholesome entertainment. But in San Francisco, when *they* take to the streets, it's a parade of homosexuals: men hugging other men, cavorting with little boys, wearing dresses and makeup."[18] Though children are not apparent in the Pride Parade footage, the commercial makes the direct claim that we "cavort with little boys." It's a grim, baseless appeal to fears of pedophilia and part of a consistent pattern invoking the civil rights of parents to "protect" children as the foundation to appeal the ordinance. By representing discrimination as an argument *for* the civil rights of parents, Bryant and Save Our Children attempted to counteract the claims made by the ordinance's supporters that it was necessary to protect the civil rights of homosexuals. In the article "The Civil Rights of Parents," Gillian Frank frames this tactic as part of a broader practice of civil rights cases opposing equity for racial and sexual minorities. She argues that the 1970s public discourse against the practice of busing to reintegrate white suburban schools laid the foundation for this public discourse on homosexuality, noting that public appeals were consistently made against busing by claiming that it infringed on the civil rights of parents to protect their children. These arguments drew on racist fears to convince voters busing Black and other racial minority students into white suburban schools would put their children at risk.[19]

This 1970s thinking can be understood through the popular refrain of the Nixon campaign about the "Silent Majority," which emboldened white suburban families to align themselves in opposition to legislation pursuing equity for racial and sexual minorities on the grounds of their own civil rights. The concept reinforced a false notion that the US class system was a meritocracy indifferent to race and that true equity would involve no action intended to improve the situations of racial and sexual minorities. Matthew D. Lassiter describes in *The Silent Majority* that "millions of white homeowners who had achieved a residentially segregated and federally subsidized version of the American Dream forcefully rejected race-conscious liberalism as an unconstitutional exercise in social engineering and an unprecedented violation of free-market meritocracy."[20] Lassiter calls this willful misinterpretation of historical reality the "'color-blind' discourse of suburban innocence," a rationale for discrimination and disenfranchisement of racial minorities predicated on ignorance of the fact that segregation resulted from tangible measures to reaffirm white America's belief in its rugged individualism and achievement while consolidating racial minorities into limited resource communities and schools.[21] Discourse opposing civil rights protections for homosexuals similarly built on a supposedly innocent narrative founded on the idea that heteronormative families faced their own civil rights infringements from ordinances protecting homosexuals from discrimination.

The success of Save Our Children and similar conservative groups furthered the political strategy of exploiting moral outrage from religious and conservative families to bring out voters and win elections. Jerry Falwell would advance the concept with the similar Moral Majority, a religious organization that he founded in 1979 seeking political influence in campaigns such as that of future president Ronald Reagan. Falwell's hatemongering included passing judgment on gay sexuality by stating things such as "Homosexuality is Satan's diabolical attack upon the family."[22] However, Falwell also sought to couch his bigotry in universalizing statements that condemned behavior (rather than people). He often insisted he bore no innate malice toward specific people or groups, remarking, "I believe that like other persons who have problems and need a change of lifestyle, homosexuals require love and help."[23] This generalizing maneuver seeks to finesse hatred and bigotry beneath a facade of alleged compassion for troubled people. When pressed about his statements regarding AIDS as a punishment for homosexual promiscuity, he contended his talk of AIDS was no different from that of other sexually transmitted infections, which he felt were God's way of "spanking us." He called "herpes, AIDS, venereal diseases, all these kinds of things . . . a definite form of the judgment of God upon society."[24] As with Bryant, who insisted her opposition to gay civil rights legislation was not bigotry but merely protection of her own rights, Falwell's statements made against homosexuals are presented as indifferent, or allegedly "compassionate," toward them. However, the surface kindness strategically masks the vindictiveness beneath it, which seeks to preserve discrimination against queers and keep schools segregated. It's this tension between an outward facade of kindness and an underlying endeavor to preserve white-only and heterosexual-only communities at all costs that resonates with the presentation of Beverly, a good upstanding, churchgoing suburban mom who just wants the perfect home and cares nothing about the lives lost in pursuit of her American dream. While Beverly's murders are not politicized as being directly antiqueer or anti-Black, they are linked repeatedly to the preservation of a Beaver Cleaver–style 1950s American ideal in which racial and sexual minorities hardly ever factor. Through her ridding the community of someone as harmless as a woman wearing white after Labor Day, we see the callousness at work in securing the white suburban American ideal at its most hyperbolic extreme.

Lee Edelman references movements such as Save Our Children, which put forth the seemingly irrefutable imperative to protect children as justification to discriminate against queer people, when articulating his antisocial position in *No Future*. He states that in the straight social order, The Child serves as "the emblem of futurity's unquestioned value" whereas the queer "comes to figure the bar to every realization of futurity."[25] Edelman advocates for the refusal of oppositional identity politics and "meaning" and for the acceptance of the burden on queerness to figure the cultural "death drive." He argues that the queer and The Child serve as oppositional markers in a social order designed to sustain futurity by displacing the death drive onto the shoulders of the queer, who signifies the failure of reproduction and violence against the future (The Child). Among the cultural images in which he locates this construction are Annie from the musical *Annie* and what he calls the "revolutionary waif" on the poster for *Les Misérables*, both of whom figure as bright, beaming bastions of hope for a future. Both shows also highlight a crucial song about the future: "Tomorrow" from *Annie* and "One Day More" from *Les Mis*. He phrases his antisocial stance against a queer oppositional politics through an indictment of the system affirmed by such figures, stating, "Fuck the social order and Child in whose name we're collectively terrorized. Fuck Annie. Fuck the waif from *Les Mis*. Fuck the whole network of symbolic relations and the future that serves as its prop."[26] It's tempting to see the slasher, a collection of films in which a queer outsider murders wholesome archetypal American teenagers, as a construction akin to Edelman's own observation of the queer as bearer of the death drive and The Child as the promise of a future under threat. However, I think there are more complex ways to respond to this connection.

Unlike slashers of the past, *Serial Mom* recognizes, in its own playful yet subversive way, that societal harm has not historically come from queers but from the entrepreneurs of the American dream. The legacy of violence and discrimination against queer people couched in wholesome, cheerful images of heterosexual families who treat us as predators and their children our prey. In 1977, a gay man in San Francisco, Robert Hillsborough, was stabbed to death in a homophobic attack.[27] Some reports alleged his killer screamed, "This one's for Anita," referring to the public face of antigay politics at the time, Anita Bryant.[28] Hillsborough's mother attempted to sue Bryant but was unsuccessful.[29] Following the attack, Harvey Milk was quoted by *The Los Angeles Times* saying that attacks on homosexuals had increased since the beginning of Bryant's campaign and that Hillsborough's murder was "only the culmination of a lot of violence that's been directed against us."[30] That same year, a gay man in Miami, John Ward, was murdered on his way home from a Pride celebration. In a 1977 pamphlet titled *Gay Liberation Today: An Exchange of Views,* John Kear reflects on these and other acts of violence affecting queer people in the wake of national antigay rhetoric paid for by Save Our Children and others, stating, "So you can see Anita Bryant's movement has produced an atmosphere of hysteria which has encouraged violent acts against the gay community."[31] In that same pamphlet, David Thorstad observes that "throughout history, homosexuals have been used as scapegoats for the ills of society—ills which homosexuals have not been responsible for."[32] These necessary observations gesture toward the tangible aftereffects of rhetoric designed to advance bias and animate bigotry toward marginalized communities. Above and beyond the already dire consequence of legislative discrimination, the weight of Anita Bryant and Save Our Children was felt in the daily lives of gay communities as a catalyst for violence, for depression and suicides. Yet the front-facing personas of these conservative movements spoke only of their love for people and their support of families with little regard for the people their actions might harm or those people's grieving families. I pose that

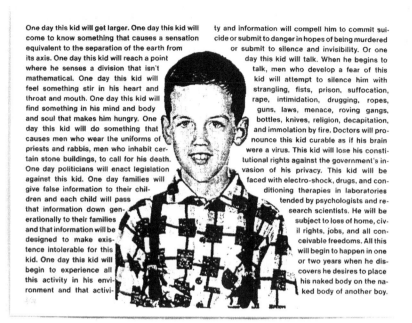

One day this kid will get larger. One day this kid will come to know something that causes a sensation equivalent to the separation of the earth from its axis. One day this kid will reach a point where he senses a division that isn't mathematical. One day this kid will feel something stir in his heart and throat and mouth. One day this kid will find something in his mind and body and soul that makes him hungry. One day this kid will do something that causes men who wear the uniforms of priests and rabbis, men who inhabit certain stone buildings, to call for his death. One day politicians will enact legislation against this kid. One day families will give false information to their children and each child will pass that information down generationally to their families and that information will be designed to make existence intolerable for this kid. One day this kid will begin to experience all this activity in his environment and that activity and information will compell him to commit suicide or submit to danger in hopes of being murdered or submit to silence and invisibility. Or one day this kid will talk. When he begins to talk, men who develop a fear of this kid will attempt to silence him with strangling, fists, prison, suffocation, rape, intimidation, drugging, ropes, guns, laws, menace, roving gangs, bottles, knives, religion, decapitation, and immolation by fire. Doctors will pronounce this kid curable as if his brain were a virus. This kid will lose his constitutional rights against the government's invasion of his privacy. This kid will be faced with electro-shock, drugs, and conditioning therapies in laboratories tended by psychologists and research scientists. He will be subject to loss of home, civil rights, jobs, and all conceivable freedoms. All this will begin to happen in one or two years when he discovers he desires to place his naked body on the naked body of another boy.

Fig 3.2 **David Wojnarowicz** *Untitled (One Day This Kid...)*, 1990 photostat and silk-screened text, copyright Estate of David Wojnarowicz.
Courtesy of the Estate of David Wojnarowicz and P·P·O·W, New York.

Beverly allegorizes much of this conservative movement and captures a heartbreaking friction at the core of gay activist dilemmas. That the public image of morality, the notions of kindness and niceness themselves, privilege whiteness, the heterosexual nuclear family, Christianity, and other cross sections of dominant cultural norms. And to pierce such power reads almost always as an affront to decency itself. Yet I want to encourage us always to pursue means that illuminate hypocrisy and call to the fore that the value of life must not be weighed with selectivity.

One such incredibly meaningful instance of this is in queer artist David Wojnarowicz's piece *Untitled (One Day This Kid...)* from 1990, just two years prior to his death from AIDS-related complications and four years before the release of *Serial Mom*. In it, he juxtaposes an image of himself as a bucktoothed child in suspenders, a visual not unlike the figures Edelman criticizes of *Annie* or *Les Mis*, with accompanying text that explains the cruel and vile ways this particular child will face physical harm and discrimination because he is queer. It calls to mind the failings of claims to "protect our children" and the ways such ideologies hypocritically perpetuate harm against some children based on discriminatory systems of value. Wojnarowicz's text contains the following.

> One day this kid will talk. When he begins to talk, men who develop a fear of this kid will attempt to silence him with strangling, fists, prison, suffocation, rape, intimidation, drugging, ropes, guns, laws, menace, roving gangs, bottles, knives, religion, decapitation, and immolation by fire. Doctors will pronounce this kid curable as if his brain were a virus. This kid will lose his constitutional rights against the government's invasion of privacy. This kid will be faced with electro-shock, drugs, and conditioning therapies in laboratories tended by psychologists and research scientists. He will be subject to loss of home, civil rights, jobs, and all conceivable freedoms. All this will begin to happen in one or two years when he discovers he desires to place his naked body on the naked body of another boy.[33]

While Edelman argues that the social order can envision queers only as antithetical to The Child (and the future), Wojnarowicz's invocation here of his own childhood locates queerness *in* the image of a child ("this kid"). He challenges the heterosexual social order that would burden the child he was in his past with death in the name of "saving" children. Most importantly, Wojnarowicz's piece, through its striking juxtaposition of image and text, identifies by name the forces that facilitated his trauma and perpetuated narratives of gay men as dangerous pedophiles, as deserving disease and death from AIDS. He does not, as Edelman suggests, remove himself from oppositional politics but instead makes a political critique that functions as a bold recognition of a moral failing.

I see a similar critique at work in Beverly's climactic murder of Mrs. Jensen in John Waters's queer slasher *Serial Mom*. I argue that the scene's appeal is twofold. That amid Beverly's attack, which comically juxtaposes the bland happiness and incessant futurity Edelman locates in *Annie* with visceral blood-splattered violence, the scene delivers a satisfying sentiment of resistance to this normative energy of perpetual futurity. It gives us that "Fuck Annie" moment Edelman uses so effectively to entice his readers. Because from the perspective of queer communities who have suffered at the expense of Save Our Children and endless invocations of The Child as a reason for our harm and discrimination, "Fuck Annie" can feel like a very valid and necessary response. However, I feel the scene does more than just that. And calling on Wojnarowicz, I'd point to how this scene importantly shifts the accountability of the violence to the systems of power that participate in our oppression. Slashers are complicated media for queer spectators because we recognize the homophobic and transphobic characterizations of gender nonconforming killers but also feel a spirit of resistance to normativity in watching them tear apart the normies. There is duality between that resistance of normativity, the "Fuck Annie" of it all, and the logical recognition that these films were made by predominantly straight artists for straight eyes, and we are maybe not their heroes. But in *Serial Mom*, we get all the indulgent potency of "Fuck Annie," of that resistant push, but we also see the responsibility for violence removed from the shoulders of queers and placed on the shoulders of heteronormative white bourgeois America. The people who have advocated against our rights, who call us pedophiles and tell us we deserve disease and death. In *Serial Mom*, we see a true naming of the power that does us harm. And so, with respect to Edelman, I say that here we have a representation that resists heteronormative futurity but also performs the political function of naming the violence against us rather than only accepting a role antithetical to society and meaning.

While Beverly conceives of her violence as bringing about her own form of white heteronormative suburban tomorrow, the future is not to be thought of as only belonging to a cis straight white bourgeoisie. In an important response to Edelman, José Esteban Muñoz poses quite oppositely that queerness is a potentiality only to be realized in a collective future and "that we are not quite queer yet, that queerness, what we really know as queerness, does not yet exist."[34] Rather than advocating for a queer exodus from oppositional politics, the social order, and meaning itself, as Edelman does, Muñoz instead poses that queerness is not "the end" but rather an ongoing future possibility, one that requires a rejection of the "here and now" and a simultaneous turn toward another time in our collective future. He observes that "the present is not enough. It is impoverished and toxic for queers and other people who do not feel the privilege of majoritarian belonging, normative tastes, and 'rational' expectations."[35] Muñoz further elaborates on the utopian potential to resolve this toxicity by considering instead how we might build collectively toward a queer utopia. For Muñoz, this principle is rooted in 1970s gay liberation wherein groups such as Third World Gay Liberation demanded a revolutionary socialist society, one that would end the notions of the bourgeois family and institutionalized religion, one that would put the needs of people first by acknowledging that land, technology, and the means of production belong to them collectively.[36] To move beyond the present, Muñoz offers that we must step outside of the restrictive logic of straight time and simultaneously envision the possibility for a queer utopia, stating "indeed to live inside straight time and ask for, desire, and imagine another time and place is to represent and perform a desire that is both utopian and queer."[37] I would like to utilize Muñoz's theory of a utopian queer future as a relevant counterpoint to Edelman's argument that the future is a tool of the heterosexual social order and consider how the climactic

"Tomorrow" murder scene in *Serial Mom* might be said to stage such a collision of ideas in a queer slasher.

There is a particularly queer temporality at play in the song "Tomorrow" itself, but this queer temporality is made more linear by the popular 1982 John Huston film adaptation. The song is notably altered in its placement and meaning by the 1982 film shown in *Serial Mom* when compared to the original Broadway show with music by Charles Strouse, lyrics by Martin Charnin, and book by Thomas Meehan. In the Broadway show, the song appears twice. In act one, it is a futile plea that introduces us to the difficult circumstance of the protagonist, Annie, who is living in an orphanage. In act two, it is reprised at a hopeful moment where genuine change seems possible. The Huston film cuts the earlier, sadder version of "Tomorrow." Instead, as is highlighted in *Serial Mom*, the song first appears as the blandly hopeful soundtrack to the opening titles and thereby nullifies its function as a plea sung by Annie in the musical's first act. The only time we see the character sing the song in the Huston film is near the end, during a scene in which Annie meets President Franklin Delano Roosevelt and single-handedly, with her sweet face and plucky attitude, inspires him to pursue the New Deal. During the Broadway version of "Tomorrow (Reprise)," there is a pivotal shift made in the lyrics of the song. In both her original rendition and the reprise of the song, Annie sings that tomorrow is "always" a day away. In the moment that Roosevelt joins her in singing, he makes the change to "only" a day away. It's a signal that he is closing the gap between the promise of a brighter future and today. Unlike the Broadway musical, the 1982 film version only ever uses the lyric "only" and never "always." The difference might seem like semantics, but it appears to posit a certain shift. "Always" implies a persistent distance from the present, that we are always one day away from tomorrow and always will be. "Only" feels imminent. It's only a day, and then tomorrow is here. It's possible to think of always as equal in meaning. That tomorrow is always a day away from today, and therefore reliable. However, "always" strikes a particularly ambivalent balance whereas "only" feels more certain. The transition between "always" and "only" in the original score, from Annie's tentative position to Roosevelt's certain optimism, indicates that this lyric transition is intended to indicate a shift in meaning, suggesting "always" was meant to be superseded in certainty with "only," and that the linguistic change is indicative of a brighter prospect.[38] The movie omits the lyric change and instead begins and stays with this brighter, hopeful version of the song, rendering it more incessantly optimistic than in the Broadway show. It presents a happy, facile version of an orphan girl on the precipice of wealth and only just a day away from a happy ending.

However, the "always" of "Tomorrow" raises deeper questions about queer temporalities. Namely that, as Muñoz describes, queerness is about living inside of straight linear time, but stepping out of it to desire another time, a collective future queer utopia. The "always" version of "Tomorrow" offers an apt expression of this experience. For queer people living in a toxic present, the potential of a queer future remains not yet here but always a day away. It is both utopian and queer to desire tomorrow, though it remains persistently in our future. In the imagining of a utopian future, there is revolutionary potential. The original lyrics to the song represent a stepping out from linear time and an exploration of queer time. One that rejects the "here and now" and simultaneously sees and explores a utopian future tomorrow, and which severs the chronological linearity of the phrase "only," as in imminently, inevitably, consistently coming. Instead, "always" suggests a constant simultaneity. That we are in the here and now and always thinking about the utopian future that stands out of chronological time as always coming but not now, not yet. It imbues the song with the deep recognition that nothing is promised, not even tomorrow. But the warm hope that when it comes, it will

Fig 3.3 The blood-splattered television screen shown at the end of Mrs. Jensen's murder to the tune of "Tomorrow" in *Serial Mom* (1994).

be liberating. In Beverly's act of murder, she performs this task of severing the certainty of tomorrow and "Tomorrow" by beating her target to death as she repeats to herself, like a mantra from the gay muses of Broadway, that tomorrow is *only* a day away, reminding her victim (and us) that to the contrary, it stands *always* a day away and is not yet here.

Edelman helps explain for me the initial appeal of the scene: the attraction of an attack on the insipidly hopeful child-obsessed heteronormative futurity seen in *Annie* and Mrs. Jensen. Wojnarowicz illuminates for me a provocative second appeal: a profound shifting of the burden of the death drive from the shoulders of the queer to the suburban housewife operating in service of bigotry to preserve a straight white capitalist suburban dream. However, it's through Muñoz that I explain the function of the scene more broadly within this book and the larger narrative of the slasher. Although Beverly, as a character, may perceive her act of murder as continuous with the hopeful affirmations of "Tomorrow," as bringing about her version of a utopia by ridding the community of "undesirable" characters, queer filmmaker John

Waters is making a substantial departure in the representation of slashers through his use of Beverly in this film. Most notably, the film indicts the politics of performative public kindness that mask private ruthlessness and harmful discrimination. It places a figure emblematic of such politics in the role of the film's central killer, breaking from a tradition of presenting the killer as queer or in some way nonnormative in their gender and sexuality. As discussed in chapter 2, Waters himself has a history of exploring queerness through radical violence, as seen in drag queen Divine's early characters such as Lady Divine in *Multiple Maniacs* (1970) and Dawn Davenport in *Female Trouble* (1974). *Multiple Maniacs* presents Divine in her form most akin to the slasher as the film's climactic sequence involves her stabbing multiple people to death before heading out with a sledgehammer to terrorize teenagers who are making out in a car. In both *Multiple Maniacs* and *Female Trouble*, Divine's characters meet grisly ends: Lady Divine is shot dead in the street by the National Guard while "America the Beautiful" plays, and Dawn Davenport is executed by electric chair. In both films, Divine's radical queer killers are punished by an outraged mainstream society and made the target of the military and the law. Conversely, *Serial Mom* concludes with Beverly Sutphin being acquitted after a lengthy trial that garners media attention, merchandising opportunities, and a movie deal with Suzanne Somers. Beverly defends herself by playing off her public image as a squeaky-clean suburban mom and manipulating each witness into incriminating themselves with some display of vulgarity. In her closing remarks, she beseeches the jury, "Look at me. I am as normal as all of you," as if her identity and social position disprove any accusation. The scene strongly differs from a similar courtroom scene at the end of *Female Trouble* in which Dawn's physical and social differences make her repulsive to the jury while the Dashers, the bourgeois couple who goaded her journey toward murder, establish distance by leaning on their own socially constructed respectability and are granted immunity. The juxtaposition demonstrates the differences between Divine's radical violence that works against social norms and Beverly's culturally sanctioned violence, which works to uphold those norms.

During Mrs. Jensen's murder, Beverly sings along with "Tomorrow" and appears to believe in the continuity between her violence and the futurity of *Annie*, including its "only" a day away belief in the linear future. However, standing outside the film, I feel instead that Beverly is enacting a contrasting irony, which is why the scene evokes an element of humor. She is not embodying a continuity. She is instead ironically counterposing the message of the song by murdering Mrs. Jensen and severing any future she has in linear time. However, in this moment the film opens an opportunity to understand a different future. One not achieved by continuity and linearity, but one conceived through queer time by simultaneity. A future that stands outside the present and is desired but not yet here. We see this in the scene as it both acknowledges a toxic present (the violence expressed by a heteronormative society in the name of preserving straight time's linear future) and simultaneously imagines a future where queerness can be found (Waters's revisionary approach to the slasher that disowns the antiqueer rhetoric of heteronormative society and instead imagines what it would be like if popular media named the right killers). Waters avows a toxic present through his portrayal of Beverly Sutphin as an enforcer of heteronormative nuclear family ideals. He further imagines another time and way of being for the slasher as a subgenre by imagining what it would be like to see a world where queers are not scapegoated as monsters, but instead their oppressors are held accountable for their discrimination and portrayed on screen not as *Leave it to Beaver* suburban nice but as depraved and ruthless in their designs for homogeneity.

At this stage in *Queer Slashers*, I begin the work of thinking through how queer filmmakers have performed and are continually performing hopeful manifestations of queer futures in their refashioning of the slasher as a horror subgenre and mass media object. I believe that it is necessary not only to feel our way through the pieces of straight media in which we can find aspects that resonate queerly but also to recognize the interventions of queer artists into these patterns. These interventions push the subgenre forward from the ideologies of an ugly past and use the template of the slasher, with its recognizable patterns and queer themes, to offer us new possibilities illustrative of a desire for queer futures that are not yet the norm of our present moment. Each of the films addressed in chapters 3 through 5 is a work by a queer filmmaker that acknowledges kinship and connection with slashers of the past but also potently imagines what the slasher can be and do for queer communities. Through analyses of these films, I make the case that in addition to looking for ourselves in the context of straight media and forging our own unconventional attachments with killers outside of heteronormative society, queer artists are challenging the structures of heteronormativity that have made us outsiders in the first place. A queer slasher is a wish for the future where we see ourselves as the subjects of the sentence and the agents of the story instead of as the shifty figures in the shadows who come to town to make their vengeance known. These films are narratives of a queer experience told through the language of one of popular cinema's most uniquely queer formulas. They are explorations of how we might reject the here and now of the slasher as it is, and the heteronormative society that made it, and simultaneously envision how the slasher could reflect the not yet hereness of queerness's future promise.

NOTES

1. There have been many other movie and TV movie versions of *Annie*, but this remains the most widely known of the bunch and is the version referenced by the Waters film. So, it will be my focus here.

2. This may also be an homage to Hitchcock's 1960 film *Psycho*, which opens with very specific time and date titles: FRIDAY, DECEMBER THE ELEVENTH and TWO FORTY-THREE P.M. Director John Waters has a long-stated love for true crime, which led him to host his own Court TV series *Til Death Do Us* Part (2007) as the Groom Reaper, who introduces and narrates reenactments of spousal murder in a mode alike to Alfred Hitchcock's hosting of *Alfred Hitchcock Presents* (1955–65).

3. The specific suburb goes unnamed in the film, but location shoots were done primarily in Towson, Maryland.

4. In the video store scene where she selects her rental, Mrs. Jensen is shown scowling at Tobe Hooper's *The Texas Chainsaw Massacre* (1974), aligning her deliberately against horror media and mediated violence.

5. This scene appears to play as an homage to an episode of *Alfred Hitchcock Presents* titled "Lamb to the Slaughter" based on a short story of the same name by Roald Dahl in which a housewife murders her husband with a leg of lamb and then feeds the murder weapon to the police investigating his murder.

6. Slasher precursors like 1945's *The Lodger* (discussed in chap. 1) also depict characters with respectable jobs that at first evade suspicion for their murders. However, they are significantly coded as nonnormative in terms of gender and sexuality, ultimately making them social outsiders.

7. John Waters, "Feature Commentary," *Serial Mom*, DVD, directed by John Waters (Universal City, CA: Focus Features, 2008).

8. John Waters, "Feature Commentary."

9. Karen Thomas, "Pee-wee Herman's Florida Misadventure," *USA Today*, July 29, 1991, 02D.

10. Claudia Feldman, "Pee-Wee Herman in Trouble—Paul Reubens' Arrest Causes Chain Reaction," *Houston Chronicle*, July 31, 1991, 1.

11. John Waters, "Feature Commentary."

12. Soren Anderson, "Review: *Serial Mom* Serves Up John Waters Wicked Wit," *News Tribune*, April 15, 1994, F4.

13. Mal Vincent, "Wacky *Serial Mom* Is a Stretch," *Virginian Pilot*, April 24, 1994, G1.

14. Vera Dika, *Games of Terror: Halloween, Friday the 13th, and the Films of the Stalker Cycle* (Madison, NJ: Farleigh Dickenson University Press, 1990), 55–56.

15. Michael Musto, "A Conversation with John Waters, the Pope of Trash," *Advocate*, November 2, 20015, https://www.advocate.com/current -issue/2015/11/02/conversation-john-waters-pope-trash.

16. Anita Bryant, *The Anita Bryant Story: The Survival of Our Nation's Families and the Threat of Militant Homosexuality* (Old Tappan, NJ: Spire, 1977), 28–29.

17. Bryant, *The Anita Bryant Story*, 87.

18. *MacNeil/Lehrer Report*, "Gay Rights," directed by Duke Struck, featuring Robert MacNeil and Jim Lehrer, aired June 6, 1977, on PBS, video and transcript made available by American Archive of Public Broadcasting, https://americanarchive.org/catalog/cpb-aacip_507 -qn5z6oct7w.

19. Gillian Frank, "'The Civil Rights of Parents': Race and Conservative Politics in Anita Bryant's Campaign Against Gay Rights in 1970s Florida," *Journal of the History of Sexuality* 22, no. 1 (January 2013): 126–60.

20. Matthew D. Lassiter, *The Silent Majority: Suburban Politics in the Sunbelt South* (Princeton, NJ: Princeton University Press, 2006), 2.

21. Lassiter, *The Silent Majority*, 1.

22. Jerry Falwell, *Listen, America!* (New York: Bantam, 1980), 159.

23. Falwell, *Listen, America!*, 161.

24. Sue Cross, "Jerry Falwell Calls AIDS a 'Gay Plague,'" *Washington Post*, June 6, 1983, B3. For similar remarks, see also "Jerry Falwell and Troy Perry Debate Morality of AIDS," *The Journal*, July 16, 1983, https://www .cbc.ca/player/play/video/1.3332889.

25. Lee Edelman, *No Future: Queer Theory and the Death Drive* (Durham, NC: Duke University Press, 2004), 4.

26. Edelman, *No Future*, 29.

27. Nicole E. Roberts, "The Plight of Gay Visibility: Intolerance in San Francisco, 1970–1979," *Journal of Homosexuality* 60, no. 1 (2013): 105–19.

28. "Anita Bryant's Clear in Gay Murder Suit," *Detroit Free Press*, November 20, 1977, 23.

29. "Judge Drops Bryant as Suit Defendant," *San Bernardino County Sun*, November 18, 1977, 33.

30. David Johnston, "S.F. Mourns Slain Gay City Worker," *Los Angeles Times*, June 25, 1977, 29, 40.

31. *Gay Liberation Today: An Exchange of Ideas* (New York: Pathfinder, 1977), 15.

32. *Gay Liberation Today*, 25.

33. David Wojnarowicz, *Untitled (One Day This Kid . . .)*, 1990.

34. José Esteban Muñoz, *Cruising Utopia: The Then and There of Queer Futurity* (New York: NYU Press, 2009), 22.

35. Muñoz, *Cruising Utopia*, 27.

36. Third World Gay Liberation (New York City), "What We Want, What We Believe," in *Out of the Closets: Voices of Gay Liberation*, edited by Karla Jay and Allen Young (New York: NYU, 1972), 363–67.

37. Muñoz, *Cruising Utopia*, 26.

38. For a discussion of how "Tomorrow" is used to convey a shift in agency, see Kevin McHugh, ed., *The Oxford Handbook of Musical Theatre Screen Adaptations* (New York: Oxford University Press, 2019), 482–85.

WHAT THE FUCK IS WRONG WITH YOU?

DURING THE CLIMAX OF THE queer horror comedy *All About Evil* (Joshua Grannell, 2010), Peaches Christ, a big-screen manifestation of the director's real-life drag character and midnight-movie hostess persona, stands toe to toe with one of the film's killers, Adrian (Noah Segan), also in drag. Adrian and his cohort of movie theater–operating murderers have trapped an audience of hundreds inside San Francisco's historic Victoria Theatre, and they're not going to let anyone out alive. Peaches's drag in the scene pays homage to the Victorian era costume of theater owner Deborah Tennis (Natasha Lyonne) as seen in a series of self-produced preshow gore films with literary pun titles such as *A Tale of Two Severed Titties*. These shorts have garnered Tennis a cult following and reinvigorated her father's failing movie business. However, viewers are unaware that these are not staged horror movies but actual filmed murders. Tennis's captive theater patrons learn the truth only as they involuntarily become the stars of her magnum opus, *Gore and Peace*. In the scene, Peaches's white corset dress is accentuated with splatters of stage blood. She also wears a pearl necklace adorned with dangling red rhinestones that resemble blood dripping from a slit throat. This playful costume tribute to Peaches's favorite screen killer dragged up with glitz and glamour contrasts Adrian's horrific drag performance as a true killer brandishing a meat cleaver in his blood-stained hands. Adrian's adoption of gender nonconforming expression as part of his performance of murderousness recalls the numerous gender nonconforming movie characters who have been portrayed as killers.[1] In chapter 2, I noted an overlap in style and performance between horror's queer killers and queer cinema's outré underground stars, comparing Leatherface's rouged human skin mask in *The Texas Chainsaw Massacre* (Tobe Hooper, 1974) to Divine's drag performance as Dawn Davenport in *Female Trouble* (John Waters, 1974). *All About Evil* might be said to further such an overlap, but it ultimately draws sharp distinctions that remind us that these histories are more a Venn diagram and less concentric circles. Importantly, in this queer-directed slasher, Adrian's killer persona and Peaches's drag persona are not merely equated but also differentiated. Peaches, following the tragic death of her sidekick Martiny, confronts Adrian with rage, asking directly and most crucially, "What the fuck is wrong with you?"

This very poignant and loaded question placed at the film's climax serves two functions. First, it is an outwardly projected question directed at Adrian, a killer in drag. In this sense, it appears to challenge the legacy of screen killers who have conflated queerness with murderousness. However, the question additionally has an introspective ring to it. It doubles as a question of the self, simultaneously affirming an overlap between the two figures and gesturing toward obvious differences. The queer horror fan asking herself about the genre, "Why do you like this?" It evokes the conflicted feelings many queer horror fans have about the genre's overlapping queer resonances and queerphobic representations.

In this chapter, I expand on the potent duality of the central question posed in *All About Evil*: "What the fuck is wrong with you?" I address how this encounter functions as a culmination of the film's examination of queer horror fandom and spectatorship. I further contextualize the film within the larger practice

Fig 4.1 Peaches Christ confronting cross-dressing killer Adrian in *All About Evil* (2010).

of Peaches Christ's multimedia drag artistry, offering ways it can be better understood in relation to her midnight-movie events and theatrical drag productions. Using queer theory about drag performance and political resistance, I attempt to explain how queer horror fans occupy a complex space as fans of a genre that commonly makes them, and their political allies in interlocking positions of marginalization, the targets of mediated violence and harmful stereotypes. Finally, I argue that *All About Evil* provides a unique exploration of the queer subject position toward horror and advocates for a fandom that both acknowledges the history of the slasher's homophobic and transphobic villains and carves out supportive queer communities organized around these ambivalent horror media.

In a 2022 episode of Peaches Christ's cult-movie podcast *Midnight Mass*, the host speaks to the ongoing sense of conflict in the life of a queer person who loves potentially exploitative horror movies. She advocates for a nuanced position that both concedes the films' foibles and respects queer attachments to horror's subversive practice of thumbing its nose at the mainstream. She also conveys that although we may not deny there is an audience for whom horror films function on a highly prurient level, there is also the possibility for media to mean more than one thing, and queer spectators like herself commonly respond differently to the material.

> There is a difference in the response to these things and the way that we view them. And so, I do say this: My fandom is different than your fandom. And I do judge their fandom a little bit because I wasn't titillated by naked women in a shower getting their bodies slashed up. That wasn't why I was tuning in to watch these movies. And I'm sorry but if you look at a lot of those films, that exploitive misogyny that is used in those films to sell tickets is why you bought a ticket. I actually am going there because I identify with the victim. I identify with the monster. I have real life fear going on because I'm getting beaten up at school because I'm a sissy. There's a few movies where you look at them and say, "OK, this is kind of a pure horror movie," but most of them I had to kind of overlook a lot of homophobia, a lot of racism, a lot of misogyny, and yet still was a fan. I still can argue that I'm a fan of these things. I think we look at something like Sleepaway Camp, we can talk about how damaging and horrible and homophobic and transphobic . . . I mean, it is awful. But yet there's still a way for me to say, "But I love that movie," and there's a reason I love it, but it gets very complicated.[2]

In a 2017 interview I conducted with Peaches, we bonded over the shared recognition that horror was one of only a select few interests common to people who grew up as sissies that also doubled as a conventionally appropriate interest for boys. In that way, Peaches remarked, going to horror conventions was something like a "beard," a rare space where queer curiosities, though not understood by peers, at least superficially overlapped with the desires of straight boys. And we could pass among them without wholly misrepresenting ourselves.

In truth, our queer engagements with the slasher were usually different from the surface-level misogyny that ignited the interests of many of our straight peers. We complexly identified with the queer outsider centered by the slasher who made the normative teens, resembling our bullies and aggressors, into his victims.[3] In our conversation, Peaches described this through her conflicted early childhood identification with Norman Bates in *Psycho* (Alfred Hitchcock, 1960): "So, it's twisted because I think part of me was frightened by Norman Bates but also that was the character I identified with. And, you know, Anthony Perkins played Norman in such a brilliant way because he wasn't necessarily overtly gay but there was definitely a queerness to him being a mama's boy and being slight. You would never describe the Norman Bates character as masculine or macho. And then, of course, we find out that he's the world's biggest mama's boy and he even dresses in drag!"[4] She went on to discuss her shift in allegiance over time from Norman Bates to the iconic slasher Freddy Krueger, who displays a comic flamboyance as he dispatches teen victims. Peaches observed that Krueger, like Bates, serves as a queer surrogate while his victims tend to stand in for the heteronormative teens who alienated her as a queer youth. Furthermore, she pointed to the queer potential of the more multidimensional survivors of the films, which she described as another character type with whom she personally identified. She compared this survivor figure to the ally women in her life who also breached heteronormativity's oppressive restrictions.

> And then, of course, because I was a sissy and I felt like an outsider as a child and identified more with girls than boys, I was ostracized, I was bullied, I was shamed. . . . As I grew up, I think, Freddy Krueger kind of replaced Norman Bates for me as a young kid because here was this killer who was overtly sassy and fabulous and horrific and could sort of torture these kids in a way that was really fun and satisfying. And often the kids that got killed in the movies first were the kids that I would have hated. It was the person who would have been my girlfriend, you know, my buddy, my feminist pal, who would always be the final scream queen.[5]

Peaches concluded that the slasher contains for her a "dual attraction" where she can "root for the protagonist as well as the killer."[6] This raises a central dilemma for queer spectators as we cope with a film formula that commonly envisions us as the killer. Though we may also root for/identify with the film's final girl, we more commonly see ourselves in the film through the figure of the killer, a cross-dressing "mama's boy" like Norman Bates or a "sassy and fabulous" child killer like Freddy Krueger. We love them and identify with them. We accept that this is a rare case where queer characters operate as powerful and radical figures of resistance to normative society. Yet we also on some level wrestle with the compromise of this position—with what it means to hold cinema's mass murderers as queer idols.

The cinematic and theatrical work of Peaches Christ offers us a broad canvas of multimedia artistry through which to understand this nuanced practice of queer spectatorship. To begin, *All About Evil* serves as an allegory for the type of horror fandom Peaches experienced as young Joshua Grannell. In the film, Steven (Thomas Dekker) is a social outsider who feels disconnected from much of the world but strongly adheres to a doting ritual of movie attendance and horror idol worship. We first meet him as a patron of Deborah's declining theater, where she greets him at the concession stand with, "The usual?" His loyalty to the theater predates the film's depiction of Deborah's rise to cult prominence. He's one of those dedicated few still going out to support single-screen independent neighborhood movie theaters. At home, we see his walls are lined with vintage horror movie posters and original drawings. He argues with his dismissive mother, Linda (Cassandra Peterson), about wanting to go to art school to major in animation. She remains unmoved by his love of horror and disapproving of his career path in the arts, remarking, "You know, I still haven't seen a Disney movie with severed heads and rotting corpses." Later, we meet Steven's friend Judy (Ariel Hart), who critiques the blatant misogyny of the gore films Steven loves.

She admits that his interest in them makes her wonder if he secretly hates women. This connection between artistic imagery and real-life intent is further expressed by Steven's English teacher, Mrs. Moorehead (Gwyneth Richards), when she confiscates a pencil drawing of the murder scene from *A Tale of Two Severed Titties* that she catches him making during class. When she questions him about it, she informs him that her concern is for the safety of her students, as she worries Steven's interests, if left unchecked, might lead to another Columbine tragedy. When Steven takes a date, Claire (Lindsy Kail), to a screening of Deborah's latest movie and she finds herself the next victim, Steven becomes a prime suspect, with Mrs. Moorehead attesting that she's had reason to be cautious about Steven's behavior for some time.

While many people in Steven's life suggest his interest in horror is a sign of malicious intent, the film itself constantly asserts the difference between Steven's artistic interests in horror and any actual violence. In this sense, he is something of a callback to Chip, Beverly's horror-obsessed son in *Serial Mom* (John Waters, 1994), and his friend Birdie, both of whom are obsessed with the genre but neither of whom means any physical harm.[7] Just as *Serial Mom* contrasted Chip and Birdie's horror fascination with Beverly's actual murders, *All About Evil* aims to differentiate Steven from Deborah's cast of killers. To this end, the encounter between Steven and Mrs. Moorehead is staged as two scenes— one in which the drawing is confiscated and another in which Mrs. Moorehead confronts Steven about it after school. Inserted between these two moments is a scene in which Deborah and her projectionist colleague Mr. Twigs (Jack Donner) first discover Adrian and recruit him as one of their band of murderers. Adrian is observed on a public sidewalk indiscriminately beating an elderly woman to death with her own cane while gleefully laughing. Placed between the two inquiries of Steven as a horror fan, the scene accentuates the differences between Steven's artistic love of horror and Adrian's outright violence. A sound bridge introducing Mrs. Moorehead's voice, beginning with the phrase "You're a smart boy, Steven," appears over the tail end of the Adrian scene, drawing the two into even closer comparison: Adrian is a violent killer whereas Steven is smart and sensitive. Just as Adrian's drag is later juxtaposed with Peaches's drag, here the joy Adrian takes in actual violence is juxtaposed with Steven's preoccupation with artistic representations of horror. It is notable that the titular question of this chapter appears twice in the film, once in the already discussed final altercation between Adrian and Peaches and once more when Steven realizes Deborah might just be a killer and not a great filmmaker. Steven is disgusted by the truth and poses, "What the fuck is wrong with you people?" The echo here affirms Steven's surrogacy to the Peaches character and further clarifies the distinct differences between artistic adoration and tangible harm. At the same time, it also forces Steven to confront that while his love of horror may be purely artistic, others exhibit perverse and violent affinities for horror. This realization echoes Peaches's podcast discussion about other forms of horror fandom that focus on the misogynist appeal of sexually objectifying and mutilating women characters.

When we spoke about the clash between Peaches and Adrian in which she asks, "What the fuck is wrong with you?" the filmmaker described this important divide between violence in art and violence in life as a core theme of the film.

> For me that movie in a lot of ways is about the difference between fantasy and reality. In that moment Peaches is realizing "You are the Columbine kids. You are an American terrorist. And I am not that. That is not what I am. I have been duped into believing you were fabulous or creative or interesting. But, no, you're just a twisted killer." So, for me, in order to make the movie work I had to set it in a world where killers could be killing and there was horror there but there is this deeper thing going on for me where I was trying to address a teenager or a drag queen's attraction to these films.[8]

I'd add that, in a way, the difference between fantasy and reality is also a core theme of this book. In chapter 1, I articulated a queer function for the slasher that involves disassembling the white bourgeois heteronormative American suburbs and adolescent stock types like jocks and prom queens through the visual metaphor of violence. A central challenge for myself, for Peaches, and for Steven is the seemingly difficult recognition that we identify with movies filled with misogynist violence and demeaning queer killers. In my work, I've often worried some part of the audience might imagine that my description of a queer function for the slasher amounts to an endorsement of mass murder, which it does not. I empathize with Steven's vulnerability to being misidentified as dangerous. And sometimes I have wondered whether this project has the value I claim. *All About Evil* knowingly leverages this self-conscious position of feeling implicated in violence to make its audience feel ill at ease with their own allegiance to Deborah. However, ultimately it breaks from the canonical slasher's common practice of inviting audiences to identify with the killer by instead offering us new avenues of queer identification in Peaches, the horror queen, and Steven, the true fan, that are still horrific and glamorous but not violent.

At the inception of Deborah's murder spree, we are positioned sympathetically toward her. Her first murder is an impulsive trauma response to the emotional and physical abuse of her cackling, demoralizing mother, Tammy (Julie Caitlin Brown), who mocks Deborah and her deceased father's dreams of being in show business. After Tammy scalds Deborah's hand and insults her with a hateful slur, Deborah snaps and stabs her mother to death in the movie theater lobby. Through a series of crossed signals and bad luck, Deborah accidentally rewires the security camera footage of the murder through the main cinema projector and replays her crime for the theater's patrons. And the audience loves it. The inciting premise of Deborah's gore filmmaking career is a desperate attempt to conceal her brutal mistake. However, slowly over time, Deborah becomes corrupted by the attention and business that her filmmaking career drives to the theater. *All About Evil* initially plays on its audience's love for cinema to make us feel complicit in cheering for the extreme measures Deborah takes to preserve the theater business, including murder. Despite this, we slowly fall out of sync with the rising star as she becomes a premeditated killer.

The film progressively diminishes the audience's ability to root for violent antihero Deborah by escalating the nature of her victims. In chapter 1, I discussed how the victims of the slasher commonly trade in stock types so paper thin you'd hardly care about their demise, citing film reviews of the period as well as Vera Dika's assertion that "these characters embody the America of the print ad, of the television commercial."[9] *All About Evil* adapts this premise for a cinephile audience, making its early victims disposable caricatures of movie theater culture's biggest villains. Deborah's first calculated murder victim, Veronica (Kat Turner), is a flagrant cell phone user. Deborah frames the culled footage of Veronica's murder as part of a preshow ad encouraging theater patrons to turn off their phones during the show, a fond sentiment in many moviegoers' minds. Another victim, Claire, is shown as a rich popular girl flanked by two minions in pink, visually recalling films such as *Heathers* (Michael Lehmann, 1989), *Jawbreaker* (Darren Stein, 1994), and *Mean Girls* (Mark Waters, 2004). When she shockingly approaches Steven in the school cafeteria, it is because of his proximity to San Francisco's newest star, Deborah. Claire is presented as a culture vulture interested in being seen at the newest trendy spot and indifferent to the fact that it's a movie theater. Once at the movie screening, Claire tries to get near Deborah to be in the frame of a local TV crew's camera. When Claire goes unnoticed, she jealously remarks that Deborah is ugly and "looks like a drag queen" (in earshot of Peaches, no less). In a final offense, the uninterested Claire disruptively stands during the show to use the bathroom, pushing past an entire row of seated patrons to reach the aisle. She meets her demise in the bathroom stall.

While these broad caricatures of bad theater patrons feel expendable in the ways that many classic slasher victims do, the film's second half introduces peril for more complex characters of value to Steven and the audience. This change in tone arrives when Steven's friend Judy sets out to interview Deborah under the pretense of a profile for the school newspaper. Once inside the Victoria Theatre, Judy slowly pieces together what is going on when she discovers Claire's distinctive sparkly pink cellphone. As Judy tries to escape through the front door, Deborah's team of murderers descends on her. The figures slowly step into the foreground of the frame, encroaching on Judy as they obstruct our view of her. Just as her face becomes fully obstructed, we hear a bloodcurdling scream. Her fate remains unclear until the film's finale, when we learn she has thankfully survived. Suspense around the *Gore and Peace* finale is also heightened by the bittersweet choice of Steven's mother, Linda, to buy a ticket, believing that she needs to finally overcome her reticence and discover once and for all what Steven likes about these movies. The film's introduction of genuine suspense and emotional stakes through the danger posed to Judy and Linda solidify a shift in audience experience from joyfully watching Deborah do away with caricatures of bad movie patrons to worrying for characters we care about. In this context, we have the final confrontation between Peaches and Adrian, which draws sharp distinctions between a fan and a killer. In the very final showdown between Steven and Deborah, during which she threatens Linda with a knife, Steven similarly admonishes Deborah for her failed fandom. Deborah reaffirms the rules of the conventional slasher, reminding Steven, "You know better than anybody, the audience is always secretly rooting for the killer." However, Steven returns that while Deborah's father "respected horror and the art of being creative," as a killer she is just a "fraud" and a "hack." The important distinction here is that filmmaking as a craft serves a creative purpose for its artists and audiences whereas murder will never be creative, and its perpetrators will always be admonished.

To better understand *All About Evil*'s nuanced portrayal of queer attraction/repulsion to horror, I want to consider it as pastiche, drawing from Richard Dyer's study of the form. Pastiche, unlike parody, does not mock its object of influence and especially emphasizes contrasting patterns of similarity to and difference from its source material. While Dyer's traits for pastiche—"likeness," "deformation," and "discrepancy"—were initially intended to describe literary pastiche, I feel these characteristics are still helpful in explaining Peaches Christ's practice of celebrating horror in a uniquely queer way that also acknowledges the genre's bleaker qualities. I begin my discussion with Christ's stage shows, which retell the plots of popular cult films with drag queens in the major roles. These shows typically function as live attractions preceding a screening of the movie. The tradition harkens back to Christ's long history of late-night movie programming. As manager of San Francisco's now shuttered Bridge Theatre (then part of the Landmark Theatres chain), Joshua Grannell created the Peaches Christ persona as hostess of the theater's movie series Midnight Mass. The drag preshow, which catered to the fans of unconventional midnight movie fare, expanded over time to become the main attraction, a full restaging of the film's plot as told by and starring the Peaches Christ drag character. Admittedly, these comedic stage adaptations would clearly not fit Dyer's criteria for pastiche as being "formally very close to what it imitates, yet it is clearly not it," as they do not bear a nearly seamless resemblance to their objects of inspiration.[10] In fact, they revel in the latter qualities of difference that Dyer ascribes to pastiche—"deformation" and "discrepancy." Therefore, by Dyer's definition, they would more likely fit into the category of homage, as they pay tribute to a work of influence without being almost indiscernible from it. However, by looking first at Christ's looser stage adaptations, I feel we can readily see those themes in Christ's oeuvre that are more subtly presented in *All About Evil*, which seems closer to a true slasher pastiche. In doing so, I hope to explain how *All About Evil* queers the slasher through the form of pastiche and how its use of pastiche elucidates the multifaceted relationship we as queer fans of horror have with this historically homophobic, transphobic, and misogynistic subgenre.

Dyer's concept of "likeness" identifies how pastiche resembles its source of inspiration yet also reframes it from a distinct perspective. He states that "pastiche imitates its idea of that which it imitates," noting that this idea "could be anything from an individual memory through a group's shared and constructed remembering to a perception current at a given cultural-historical moment."[11] While Christ's stage shows are notably different from their sources of inspiration in tone, casting, and medium of delivery, they demonstrate Peaches's practice of presenting her queer San Francisco audience with a vision of the films they love from the vantage point of contemporary San Francisco queer culture. The appeal of her shows is rooted in mutual appreciation by the queer artist and audience for a shared point of reference. In describing her creative process, Peaches notes that she primarily seeks to harvest from a script those recognizable moments—bits of dialogue, musical numbers, stunts or gags—that fans idolize and associate most strongly with the film. She says, "I have to watch it over and over again. I have to break it down. I tear the plot apart. I decide what needs to stay, what needs to go. What's important to a cult movie audience? What are the moments that I have to celebrate on stage? And then how do I queer it and repurpose it?"[12] Here, Peaches alludes simultaneously to what is like the film (those iconic moments fans want) and what is different (the queer turn toward drag and gay culture). Especially important is the identification that Peaches's target audience enters already knowing the references. Her adaptation process focuses on what a cult audience of obsessives will want to see, and her goal is to celebrate with reverence these indelible elements of the film.

In fact, Peaches's stage shows often rely on the audience's fervent knowledge of the movie to fill in gaps. These shows are tasked with transforming the qualities of edited film into a series of stage vignettes limited to a few key settings, with sets scaled down to painted cardboard backdrops and sometimes only the verbal cue of a prop. An example of this playful practice of verbally cueing the audience to imagine aspects of the film that are too complex to stage can be seen in *The Witches of Eastbay*, when Peggy Leggs approximates an elaborate stunt from *The Witches of Eastwick* (George Miller, 1987) in which Veronica Cartwright as Felicia (Fellatio, in the stage show) slips on pearls strewn about the floor and falls down a flight of stairs. In this case, Fellatio shuffles her feet across the bare stage and announces, "Slipping on pearls! Slipping on pearls!" before contorting her body down the stage right steps to indicate a tumble.[13] This incident is representative of the whimsical homage seen in Peaches Christ's stage productions. They pay tribute to their source material by staging a version of the film's plot as retold through the medium of a drag show. This crucial addition innately modifies the structure of the film since, as a drag show, there is the need to stage choreographed lip-sync performances within the plot of the movie. Sometimes the shows work drag numbers into already existing moments of musical performance from the film such as the talent show performance of "Jingle Bell Rock" in *Mean Girls* (now *Mean Gays*) or the Motown girl-group medley that opens *Sister Act* (Emile Ardolino, 1992, now *Mister Act*). Other times, the numbers are new additions used primarily to demonstrate the performing talents of the featured queens. What you get in a Peaches Christ show are recognizable characters, costumes, and plot from the film but reimagined for the stage of San Francisco's Castro Theater and Peaches' cast of queens. However, nothing about the stage show is identical in style or form to the original.

Christ meaningfully engages in transformative work that I'd like to think of in terms of what Dyer calls "deformation."

Dyer argues that pastiche "deforms the style of its referent: it selects, accentuates, exaggerates, concentrates."[14] By selecting and emphasizing certain traits, pastiche "makes the trait appear more present and insistent than it was in the original." In a Peaches Christ production, those traits tend to be elements of the original film with a distinctly queer and camp sensibility that her audience may have read into more, or interpreted differently, than a straight mainstream movie audience would. A common example of this is the embellished horniness in Peaches' shows, which commonly take a moment of mild eroticism or sexual subtext from a film and exaggerate it to comic effect. For example, a scene from *The Witches of Eastwick* in which leading ladies Susan Sarandon, Cher, and Michelle Pfeiffer giggle about their ideal man's penis size is given added sexual glee in *The Witches of Eastbay*. Coco Peru, in the Sarandon role, repeats a verbatim line from the film's script that counters the size-queen dialogue with "I prefer small." However, Coco one-ups this by lapsing into a heated fervor, imagining her lover's penis slapping her about the face and moaning, "Si papi, si papi, who's your Coco? Who's your Coco, papi?" (a reference to Coco's tendency to brag about her handsome Spanish husband). The scene selects a small moment of frank sexual conversation from the film and exaggerates it into a more prevalent exploration of queer sexual desire. Similarly, in a comedic moment during *Return to Grey Gardens*, a stage version of the documentary *Grey Gardens* (Albert and David Maysles, 1975), Peaches, in the Big Edie role, exaggerates a scene in which Big Edie boasts that local gardener Jerry likes how she "does her corn." In the Peaches version, she makes this speech while slathering a corn cob with butter and gliding her hand up and down it to simulate masturbation.[15] The undercurrent of sexual innuendo in the corn speech in the film becomes a brazen, sexual joke that elevates those elements that queer audiences, and especially audiences of gay men, may have picked up on and emphasized in their minds.

Perhaps the most fruitful of Dyer's criteria for pastiche with regards to the Peaches Christ stage shows is that of "discrepancy," which includes "inconsistent or inappropriate" aspects of a text, such as extraneous elements, anachronistic language, and self-reference by the author. These moments of discrepancy reinforce the style of the original text by emerging from it to call attention to what it is not.[16] A Peaches Christ production is not a seamless facsimile of the original film but instead a restaging that accentuates anachronistic references to contemporary queer life in San Francisco and extraneous inside jokes about its drag queen stars. The shows also celebrate at every turn opportunities for line flubs and stage gaffes, making a show within the show all about if and how this production will get finished. In the end, a Peaches Christ show is about the staging of a Peaches Christ show as it's happening in the room. All her shows are set in whatever venue the show is being held. *Return to Grey Gardens* alleges that Peaches and Jinkx Monsoon have been squatting in the Castro Theatre since the show started forty years earlier, mirroring the isolated recluses of the film's titular home. *The Witches of Eastbay* refers to the San Francisco Bay Area. However, when Christ restaged the show in New York, it was reimagined as *The Witches of East Village* (referring to Manhattan's East Village neighborhood).[17] The shows remain amorphous and in flux, open to improvisations that fit the location and cast. In a Peaches Christ show, we are always seeing the plot of the film but as rewritten for the day. For the place we are, the people on stage, and the people in the audience.

Among the most fascinating results of this fluidity is the celebration of the queer performers in the major roles, who do not disappear into a character but are instead always presented with a script tailored to their specific casting. The shows commonly begin with an opening title sequence that plays on a video screen above the stage. These credits blend elements of the original film's opening credits with custom elements referencing the stage show. This includes glamour photos of each of the show's marquee stars as their drag characters, not as the film characters. In this way, the show always emphasizes the stars themselves, who occupy positions equivalent to recognizable film characters without ever playing those specific roles by name. The composite stage character is at once the drag performer, the film character, and the original actor who played that character, with the show oscillating between elements of these three figures. Christ describes this as "channeling more than one cult," meaning that she is playing to her audience's queer love for the drag performer just as much as for the film character and the leading lady who played her in the movie.[18] For example, drag performer Chad Michaels, a renowned Cher impersonator, plays Chad as Cher as Alexandra, Cher's character from *The Witches of Eastwick*, but as if Chad, the drag queen, were faced with her circumstances. This includes allusions to Chad's life and career, such as jokes about her being the winner of *RuPaul's Drag Race All Stars* as well as in-jokes about Alexandra's plotline in the movie and references to Cher's decades-long multimedia career. We see this in nods to Cher's past films and songs, including an obligatory "snap out of it!" (from her Oscar-winning turn in John Patrick Shanley's 1987 film *Moonstruck*) and a musical medley of "Dark Lady" and "If I Could Turn Back Time." A key accomplishment of this style of stage homage is that the queer performers are never made to disappear into a role or asked to play a straight character. The queens in Peaches's shows play their own drag characters while also paying tribute to the films and their actresses. This remedies the invisibility of queer people, who are virtually nonexistent in the tributed films.

In fact, in a Peaches show, nearly every character is a drag queen or gay man. The plots of the films are also transformed into crises facing drag queens and queer people. *Hocus Pocus* (Kenny

Ortega, 1993) is a film about three witches, the Sanderson sisters, who drink the souls of children to achieve immortality. *Hocum Pokem* reimagines the film as a show about drag queens who, facing harsh beauty standards in their industry, suck the life out of young queens to preserve their youthful appearance. In one scene, BenDeLaCreme in the Kathy Najimy role, Mary, channel surfs on a 1990s television and flips past TV infomercials to see footage of Bill Clinton discussing the newly passed military policy "Don't Ask, Don't Tell."[19] This choice interjects the decade's queer political challenges into the show, referencing what queer audiences of the film were experiencing outside the theater doors during the time of its release. It serves as a pointed reminder of how these media we adore exclude us and fail to address those issues we experience unique from the straight family audiences they prioritize. However, Peaches's versions of these films bring the social and political struggles of queer people to the forefront, bending the films' plots to fit queer life in San Francisco. In her versions of these films, it is straight people who are invisible. Every corner of the theater belongs to us.

As I reflect on the larger purpose for the Peaches Christ stage shows, I find among the most important to be the creation of queer community. These are works by queer artists in which queer characters abound, where queer audiences see themselves in their favorite films for the first time as they are all newly about queer folks in San Francisco. It is crucial to note Peaches Christ's work is not mere idol worship but about forming a queer chosen family around homage to queer artists and cult movies.

The development of queer community around cinematic exhibition has deep roots stretching back to the countercultural and underground cinema of the 1960s. Janet Staiger writes in *Perverse Spectators* that in the early 1960s, "midnight cinema was . . . an expression of community and a site for community building."[20] One that played a pivotal role in the development of a gay liberation culture that criticized heteronormative gender and sexuality. She also contextualizes the films' cinematic reiterations of gay culture and popular media as an integral part of both their critique of heteronormativity and their community building among gay audiences. Staiger states that "ironic appropriations of popular culture were stylistic tactics directed against bourgeois culture but also assertive rhetorical strategies for creating these subcultural community connections."[21] Often, screening events were pretense for gay social gatherings and created a phenomenon of cinematic overflow, stretching into the night and expanding out into the street. An excellent example of a communal organization blossoming into a grassroots cinematic community can be found in the Gay Girls Riding Club, a social group for gay men in Los Angeles that created a series of drag homage films during the 1960s and '70s. Perhaps most relevant to the Peaches Christ oeuvre are *What Really Happened to Baby Jane?* (Connie B. De Mille, 1963) and *All About Alice* (Ray Harrison, 1972), drag versions of *What Ever Happened to Baby Jane?* (Robert Aldrich, 1962) and *All About Eve* (Joseph L. Mankiewicz, 1950), respectively. Christ staged the former as *What Ever Happened to Bianca Del Rio?* (renamed for its title star) and used the latter's title as inspiration for *All About Evil*. The Gay Girls Riding Club films are played relatively straight, following the memorable beats of their filmic inspiration with small, notable differences that invoke gay culture of the time. In *Coming Together*, Ryan Powell describes their filmmaking practice as documenting the landscape of '60s gay life, especially the Southern California locales the Gay Girls Riding Club frequented, as well as reimagining their lives through the lexicon of Hollywood cinema. He describes how "using real locations, many of them highly public, the Gay Girls Riding Club created films that explicitly placed gay male sociality—including both same-sex coupling and dissident gender performance—a part of both actual city space and within the terms of popular imagery of Hollywood movies."[22] While the films are highly faithful to their source material, moments of variation tend to be loaded with nods to their intended audience of gay men. In their *Baby Jane* homage, the rat Jane serves to Blanche is instead a flaming food tray. Powell notes this to be a visual pun suggesting the drag version of Blanche (played by Roz Berri) is a "flaming queen."[23]

Christ cites another communal group of artists and performers with cinematic roots, the Cockettes, as inspiration for her move to San Francisco. The Cockettes were a multiracial, gender nonconforming, philosophically heterogeneous, and frequently naked avant-garde collective of the 1970s whose eclectic body of work spanned stage and screen. They began as part of the midnight movie series Nocturnal Dream Shows at the Palace Theater, emerging to perform an impromptu kick line in the style of Radio City Music Hall's famous dancers the Rockettes (who also inspired their name). With time, their stage shows expanded in length and ambition. Of relevance to Christ's work are their reiterations of Hollywood films, such as the stage show *Gone with the Showboat to Oklahoma*. As might be expected, the show combined elements of Hollywood features *Gone with the Wind* (Victor Fleming, 1939), *Show Boat* (George Sidney, 1951), and *Oklahoma!* (Fred Zinnemann, 1955), the latter two of which were based on Broadway musicals of the same name. Malik Gaines describes in *Black Performance on the Outskirts of the Left* how "in these collapsed genre pieces, an intertextual strategy becomes evident ... intervening against a text's norms by ridiculously reenacting it."[24] The show restaged Hollywood films that represented fallacious and racist imagery of Black and Indigenous communities. However, according to Gaines, the Cockettes' "parodic interpretation of these genres emphasizes the fictitiousness of these claims."[25] This work of imbuing Hollywood cinema with elements of contemporary gay life and the use of pastiche's discrepancy to stress the films' failures to accurately represent marginalized communities both speak to Peaches Christ's theatrical history of turning cult movies into communal stage shows that populate recognizable plots with queer characters for queer audiences.

In Dyer's account of pastiche, he notes a particular usefulness for the form in representing the otherwise overlooked communal engagements with a source text held by marginalized communities. In one cinematic application of pastiche, Dyer reflects on the form's purpose by considering queer filmmaker Todd Haynes's 2002 film *Far from Heaven*, which pastiches Douglas Sirk's *All That Heaven Allows* (1955) by creating a period melodrama with nearly identical cinematography and style to Sirk's 1950s film that includes queer and interracial relationships not present during the restrictive era of the Production Code. He reflects on how the modern Haynes film, through its overlapping aspects of likeness and difference to the '50s Sirk film, invites audiences to experience an emotional connection with the past while also reinforcing an understanding that everything we know about the past is learned through media. He suggests that this connects us to an understanding of the structures of feeling we have inherited. That by recognizing a mediated emotional connection with the past, we realize our present is also a historicized structure through which we see everything. He argues of pastiche, "It is social: it always accepts and indicates what is really the case in all cultural production, that it exists by virtue of the forms and frameworks of meaning and affect available to it."[26] Dyer argues that cognizance of the frameworks under which we experience and understand media can be "especially congenial to social groupings or individuals within them who feel marginal" as "it affirms the position from which it is produced."[27]

Drawing on Dyer's reading of *Far from Heaven*, I argue that the effect of Christ's stage shows, which re-present the recognizable plots of cult films is twofold: (1) They concentrate and emphasize those elements of the original films that speak to contemporary queer communities, particularly among the queer scene of San Francisco. They affirm to an audience of queers that the queer stance we have taken toward these films has a shared collective presence, intervening into the potential to feel our queer meanings are alien or "alternative." In a Peaches Christ production, queer expressions of joy are the norm. (2) They simultaneously emphasize, by their concentration and exaggeration of what feels queer about the original work, that the work itself was never innately queer. Christ's stage performances make apparent the framework of heteronormativity under which queer fascinations are formed. Her infusions of the film's plot with gay characters, drag queens, queer political issues, and inside jokes about the Castro show us what a historically specific queer work of art looks like. This calls to mind how none of the original films told queer stories or acknowledged our historical existence. And so, we at once see our queer love of these films honored and become acutely aware through the queering of the films on stage that they were always objects able to be queered, not made for us but made queer by us. That as potent and beautiful as the queer surrogacy of Little Edie and the Sanderson sisters might be, this surrogacy was formed under the framework of heteronormativity that perpetually disenfranchised and eradicated queer youth. We saw ourselves in the films most available to us because authentically queer media generally was not.[28] The collective of shared recognition born under the roof of the Castro Theatre is a bond forged as much over what we have as over what we don't have. We have these films we can join around and affirm our queer experiences with, but we also see in the room a cohort of queer gatherers feasting on the scraps of a social order not designed for them, where they are tasked with seeing themselves in something not made with them in mind. It's a communal acknowledgment of both presence and lack.

This ambivalence informs my understanding of how drag and pastiche work dually in *All About Evil* to affirm queer attachments to horror while also exhibiting an awareness of how heteronormativity shapes those affections. Judith Butler argues in *Bodies That Matter* that drag works complexly by representing oppressive norms of sex, race, and gender in ways that allow queer performers to manage their relationship with those ideological tools of oppression by the very act of their repetition. However, there is never an ability to completely escape the structures of meaning we are born into. She draws here on Louis Althusser's theory of interpellation, noting the example of the police officer who hails an individual as "Hey, you there!" which yields a response of the individual turning their attention toward the police officer, thereby interpellating them as a subject.[29] Althusser discusses what he calls the Ideological State Apparatuses that often collaborate to facilitate compliant conduct by those individuals interpellated as subjects under an ideology, often with the belief that their adherence to this conduct is a chosen part of their free will. Thus, ideology is "purely imaginary," an unenforced mandate of being, yet exists primarily in the tangible subjects who operate in its service.[30] Further, Althusser considers that subjects "always-already are" as the ideological imaginings for the unborn conceive of them in terms of the ideology that awaits them after their birth, projecting onto unborn offspring ideas of what they already are and will be.[31] The Ideological State Apparatuses that Althusser identifies, including the interlocking efforts of church, school, and family, reflect those institutions identified by post-Stonewall gay liberation activism as sustaining queer oppression (discussed in chap. 1) and against which Eve Sedgwick defines queerness (seen in her characterization of Christmas in chap. 2). While we might hope and imagine this nexus of indoctrination could be challenged by queer subjects who speak against the ethical and legal sanctions used to support an oppressive ideology, Althusser's theory that ideology invisibly sustains itself as an eternal structure maintained under the subject's perceived free will problematizes the available positions for resistance.

Drag, for Butler, is one site to open up reworkings of this ideological structure, though ultimately an ambivalent one. She argues that drag as documented in *Paris Is Burning* (Jennie Livingston, 1990) "both appropriates and subverts racist, misogynist, and homophobic norms of oppression" and that notably "some-times it is both at once."[32] Drag does not fully disassociate the subject from the inescapable ideology into which they have been interpellated, as they must innately utilize the language of the ideology itself in their articulations of their opposition to it. In-stead, Butler argues that "the citing of the norm does not displace that norm; rather, it becomes the means by which that norm is most painfully reiterated as the very desire and the performance of those it subjects."[33] She calls this, appropriately enough for drag, a "make over" or "a making over which is itself a kind of agency, a power in and as discourse, in and as performance, which repeats in order to remake."[34] In the case of Peaches Christ's drag, I would add that in addition to those norms of sex and gender being reworked, those oppressive tropes perpetuated by media of queers as mentally ill, as criminals, as killers are also among the norms getting a "make over," or being reiterated by the perfor-mance of the queer artist to achieve a form of agency and power within them. Dressed as Freddy Krueger or Hannibal Lecter, Peaches both appropriates and subverts the legacy of queer kill-ers. It is at once a celebration of the child who identified vividly with Norman Bates and an admonishment of the ideology that made that his only point of identification. The norms are reiter-ated, and they continue, but moments of rupture that hope to subvert them exist.

To return to the beginning, to "What the fuck is wrong with you?" as an interrogation of the queer killer canon and also of the queer self in killer drag, I want to understand the ways in which drag and pastiche work together in *All About Evil* to express a queer position that both appropriates, or accepts the place of queerness in the history of the slasher's killers, and subverts, or gives this history a "make over." I'll also be using those practices of drag seen in Christ's stage shows to help direct my focus on the film's elements of pastiche, connecting *All About Evil* to Peaches's parallel career of theatrical drag productions. In a way, I want to propose that *All About Evil*, as cinematic pastiche, is a mediated form of drag performance, accentuating aspects of likeness to the canonical slasher as well as utilizing moments of rupture to subvert and point out the style of those originals. *All About Evil* as queer slasher pastiche processes the painful history of the slasher in a similar way drag does a history of ideologically reinforced gender norms, by deriving power through the reiteration of the hurtful trope of the queer killer by those it has degraded. While this does not end or undo the trope itself, it affords queer performers and filmmakers a space through which to restage the trope, achieve a kind of agency within it, and potentially subvert some of its vitriolic legacy. A queer exploration of the slasher, however redemptive and celebratory, bears an inexorable trace of pain. It is always an ambivalent position that takes on a homophobic and transphobic past while navigating one's way through the mire toward a sense of agency and mastery over the visual language we have inherited.

All About Evil tells its story of meek movie theater owner turned media-hungry murderer Deborah Tennis as refracted through a prism of queer, cult, horror, and slasher cinema. This begins with its title, a slant on the gay classic *All About Eve* (1950), which mirrors Christ's theater practice of staging shows with pun titles that transform the original into something queerer, dirtier, or draggier. There also exists a kind of crooked parallel between Tennis and Anne Baxter's Eve Harrington as both rise from humble beginnings and cunningly propel themselves into stardom. The film begins with a flashback to Deborah's childhood performance as Dorothy at a kids' matinee of *The Wizard of Oz* (Victor Fleming, 1939), where she is accidentally electrocuted after she nervously urinates on exposed stage wiring. Her mother laughs maniacally at Deborah's pain while dressed in character as Margaret Hamilton's Wicked Witch of the West. In addition to the movie reference to *Oz*, the scene follows a common slasher pattern by opening with a flashback scene of trauma that incites and motivates the film's central killer.[35] Commonly, though not always, this has been a childhood scene as in *Homicidal* (William Castle, 1961), *Sleepaway Camp* (Robert Hiltzik, 1983), or, perhaps most memorably, *Halloween* (John Carpenter, 1978). The scene concludes with the revelation that Deborah has been permanently marked by the incident with a streak of gray hair. This visually recalls a similar streak that develops for Nancy (Heather Langenkamp) after an attack by Freddy Krueger in *A Nightmare on Elm Street* (Wes Craven, 1984). Later, when Deborah murders her derisive mother, she proclaims, "Oh god, mother, blood!" while caressing her blood-soaked face. The line is a verbatim homage to what Norman Bates (Anthony Perkins) says after his mother returns to the Bates' home following the shower murder of Marion Crane (Janet Leigh) in *Psycho* (1960). Norman's mother, of course, is really him dressed as his mother in what Peaches calls "drag." Deborah and Norman share a similarly tempestuous entwinement with a mother figure whom they eventually murder and whose demise begins each killer's spree. Together this set of references speaks to a collective memory, or "likeness," kaleidoscopically representing past media in a new form. The film invokes the slasher and its predecessors to establish a connection with those prior works. Therefore, its later departures derive meaning in the ways they deviate from the slasher's common conventions. *All About Evil* is a movie about film lovers as told with reverence to a cinematic past that also reshapes the slasher's historical relationship with queer killers by reiterating this trope from a queer perspective.

All About Evil advances this queer perspective through its elements of discrepancy, which emphasize anachronistic and self-referential aspects of the film that differentiate it from the canonical slasher. A common convention of Peaches's stage shows that we see again in *All About Evil* is the use of the composite character who signals more than one thing to an audience. Particularly, the recognition that the performer on screen is a character in the film but also exists within a larger media context at the same time. Cassandra Peterson is best known for playing the macabre movie hostess Elvira, Mistress of the Dark, in a decades-long career that spans a wide array of media. However, here she plays Steven's mother, Linda. In one scene, Linda tries to reconcile with her horror-obsessed son, and the very touching dramatic scene plays out with a poster showcasing a voluptuous swimsuit-clad Elvira in plain view above Steven's bed. During a moment when Steven remarks that he thinks he's in love with an older woman, an eye-line match directs us to Linda's gaze at the poster, as if suggesting Elvira were the target of his desire. The effect is not entirely unlike the opening titles of a Peaches stage show where the marquee drag stars are shown on screen as their drag characters while the show itself situates them in specific character roles. We are alerted to the idea that Cassandra Peterson is at once in this scene Cassandra, Linda, and Elvira—a performer, a movie character, and a drag icon. The decision also adds a touch of perversity to the scene by suggesting something vaguely incestuous about horror-loving Steven and his adoration of Elvira given her simultaneity as his mother, Linda. This plays to a queer eye as a kinky in-joke among audiences attune to the duality innate to Peterson's casting. It also underlines a redemptive stroke of queer intervention here that speaks to the concurrent celebration of the Elvira character and urge to subvert or introduce variance into Peterson's legacy. The noted difference here is, of course, Elvira as poster model is a commodity of sexual objectification. But by expanding Peterson's range of presentation further, allowing her to be both horror bombshell and concerned mom at the same time, Christ challenges limitations that heteronormative horror often places on women.[36] As a form of femme drag, the Elvira character already appropriates and subverts norms about sex and gender projected onto women. She embodies a hypersexual ditzy persona common in media but, through reiteration of these norms, creates space for agency to be claimed. This is a key instance where the performance of drag layers over the film's

Fig 4.2 Cassandra Peterson as Steven's mom, Linda, in *All About Evil* (2010) sitting in front of a pinup poster of herself as Elvira, Mistress of the Dark, hung above Steven's bed.

pastiche, creating multiple variables that appropriate gender and genre norms while also achieving subversion through repetition and differentiation.

Perhaps the most complex and widely variable screen presence at work in the film is that of Peaches Christ herself. As writer/ director Joshua Grannell, whose name we see splashed across the opening credits. In surrogate form as Steven, a young outcast and film lover obsessed with horror, cult movies, and classic movie theaters.[37] Peaches as Peaches Christ, a cinematic version of her own drag character living and working in San Francisco. *All About Evil*, like her stage productions, remains a historically and geographically specific queer work of art, set in the place and time of Peaches's own midnight movie career. In the world of *All About Evil*, Deborah is something of a contemporary to Peaches, another cult star birthed from the San Francisco movie scene. Perhaps most dire of all, Peaches is also reflected on screen in her most cynical form through Deborah. Christ's filmmaking career began with short films used as preshow material for

Midnight Mass that told variations of popular film plots with drag characters. These underground shorts, not unlike Deborah's gore films, became a part of the promotion for the movie events they accompanied and garnered an audience all their own. One such film, *A Nightmare on Castro Street* (2002), imagines drag performer Squeaky Blonde as a Freddy Krueger-esque killer who stalks and kills local San Francisco queens Heklina and Martiny. The film re-creates key moments of *Nightmare* but augments them for drag, such as a scene that reimagines the famous shot of Krueger's finger razors between Nancy's legs in the bathtub with sharp purple fingernails. Deborah seems to represent a worst-case scenario, or a bizarro doppelgänger to Christ's own career as a theater manager who used horror shorts to promote her movie programming. With the film's central arc imagining how far one might go to save the cinema.

All About Evil is an act of cinematic drag, a pastiche of the canonical slasher that reiterates its tropes to achieve a kind of agency within them. This composite presentation of Peaches Christ on screen at once as Peaches, Steven, and Deborah emulates her stage practice of playing, for example, Peachy Manderson (Peaches as Bette Midler as Winnie Sanderson) in *Hocum Pokem*. We see through the craft of filmmaking and the art of drag an individual as more than one thing at a time, never limiting them to a single role in the film but allowing them multiplicity on screen. The conversation in which Steven confronts Deborah as a fraud can be seen, then, as an internal conversation between Peaches as earnest teenage fan and Peaches as business owner, entrepreneur, and empresario of midnight movie events. It's a message from and to the self that serves as a guiding light to always honor art and creativity and to never succumb to ego and ruthless self-interest. Likewise, the final confrontation between Peaches, in full horror drag, and Adrian, a true killer in drag, stages a conversation between Peaches, the cultivator of drag stage shows that build queer community around cult films, and the embodiment of the slasher's queer killers in which we often see ourselves but by which we also feel villainized. Peaches, the drag character, dressed as killer Deborah, embodies drag's ability to appropriate the norms with which we have been oppressed. To take on both the gender role of the femme, or sissy, and the genre role of the queer killers young Peaches identified with such as Norman Bates. However, it's in her act of rejecting Adrian that drag challenges the genre's norms. As Peaches says, "what the fuck is wrong with you?" is a statement that "you are an American terrorist. And I am not that."[38] It embraces a position within the ideology of queer killer films that can be used to build community and foster queer relationships but rejects the violent aftermath, the legacy of ridicule and harm. Or, at least, hopes to dispel it. Not unlike in *The Wizard of Oz* when the pretty pink bubble witch Glinda snarks to the Wicked Witch of the West, "Begone, before somebody drops a house on you too" (a delineation between two types of witches). As *All About Evil* is itself an act of cinematic drag through pastiche, its elements of gender and genre work dually to appropriate norms and reiterate them to achieve power within them, and perhaps even subvert them.

A queer slasher is ultimately an invocation of an oppressive past that utilizes this inherited language as a form through which to explore and understand the position of queers within the slasher from a newly queer vantage point. Through this practice, queer filmmakers employ a subgenre in which they were commonly made predators and killers to see and understand themselves, bending the subgenre in the process with aims to appropriate but also subvert. "What the fuck is wrong with you?" carries the weight of both aims. It interrogates the queer self in their complicity with the appropriation of cinema's homophobic and transphobic norms. But also, it looks at the slasher subgenre and poses a potentially empowering question about what is wrong with it and how it could be changed for the better. Through the appropriation of the canonical slasher's tropes, the queer slasher begins the work of understanding our place within the subgenre's history. By deviating from the form to make apparent its past foibles, it creates moments of subversion that speak to our ambitions to see more for ourselves on the horizon.

NOTES

1. See chapter 1's discussion of the queer lineage of the slasher.

2. Peaches Christ and Michael Varrati, "Episode 23: Creature from the Black Lagoon," February 16, 2022, *Midnight Mass*, produced by Peaches Christ Productions, podcast audio, 1:47:43, https://midnightmass .buzzsprout.com/1796691/10070643-episode-23-creature-from-the-black -lagoon.

3. See chapter 1's discussion of the queer function of the slasher.

4. Joshua Grannell (Peaches Christ) in conversation with the author, August 26, 2017.

5. Joshua Grannell (Peaches Christ) in conversation with the author, August 26, 2017.

6. Joshua Grannell (Peaches Christ) in conversation with the author, August 26, 2017.

7. See chapter 3 for further discussion of this film.

8. Joshua Grannell (Peaches Christ) in conversation with the author, August 26, 2017.

9. Vera Dika, *Games of Terror:* Halloween, Friday the 13th, *and the Films of the Stalker Cycle* (Madison, NJ: Farleigh Dickenson University Press, 1990), 55–56.

10. Richard Dyer, *Pastiche* (New York: Routledge, 2007), 59.

11. Dyer, *Pastiche*, 55.

12. Peaches Christ and Michael Varrati, "Episode 30: Drop Dead Gorgeous," April 6, 2022, *Midnight Mass*, produced by Peaches Christ Productions, podcast audio, 1:35:57, https://midnightmass.buzzsprout .com/1796691/10384527-episode-30-drop-dead-gorgeous.

13. Peaches Christ Productions, *The Witches of Eastbay*, Castro Theater, San Francisco, archival performance video.

14. Dyer, *Pastiche*, 56.

15. Peaches Christ Productions, *Return to Grey Gardens*, Castro Theatre, San Francisco, archival performance video.

16. Dyer, *Pastiche*, 58.

17. Glenn Garner, "Peaches Christ Serves a Wicked Parody of *The Witches of Eastwick*," *Out*, April 4, 2016, https://www.out.com/entertainment /2016/4/04/peaches-christ-serves-wicked-parody-witches-eastwick.

18. Joshua Grannell (Peaches Christ) in conversation with the author, August 26, 2017.

19. Peaches Christ Productions, *Hocum Pokem*, Castro Theatre, San Francisco, archival performance video.

20. Janet Staiger, *Perverse Spectators: The Practices of Film Reception* (New York: New York University Press, 2000), 126.

21. Staiger, *Perverse Spectators*, 126.

22. Ryan Powell, *Coming Together: The Cinematic Elaboration of Gay Male Life, 1945–1979* (Chicago, IL: University of Chicago Press, 2019), 53.

23. Powell, *Coming Together*, 54.

24. Malik Gaines, *Black Performance on the Outskirts of the Left: A History of the Impossible* (New York: New York University Press, 2017), 149.

25. Gaines, *Black Performance*, 151.

26. Dyer, *Pastiche*, 179.

27. Dyer, 179.

28. For discussions of the queer relationship to straight media in childhood, see Eve Sodofsky Sedgwick's discussion of how we "smuggle" our childhood fascinations into our writing and research as queer scholars in *Tendencies* (Durham, NC: Duke University Press, 1993), 3. See also Michael Moon's discussion of queer boys as "hyper mimetic" or "imitation women" whose queerness first expresses itself in childhood through the emulation of famous actresses rather than same-sex attraction in *A Small Boy and Others: Imitation and Initiation in American Culture from Henry James to Andy Warhol* (Durham, NC: Duke University Press, 1998), 9.

29. Louis Althusser, *Lenin and Philosophy, and Other Essays* (New York: Monthly Review, 2001), 118.

30. Althusser, *Lenin and Philosophy*, 108.

31. Althusser, 119.

32. Judith Butler, *Bodies That Matter: On the Discursive Limits of Sex* (New York: Routledge, 1993), 128.

33. Butler, *Bodies That Matter*, 133.

34. Butler, 137.

35. For Dika's complete description of the "stalker film," her category of tales of terror that overlaps with the canonical slasher, including these "past-event" opening scenes, see *Games of Terror*, 53–63.

36. In conversation with Peaches Christ, Elvira describes being typecast during her time with improv troupe tThe Groundlings: "My

characters were always kind of the same character over and over: sexy, actress, hooker, stripper, showgirl. I got kind of pigeonholed in that." Of her role in *All About Evil*, she offers, "It was so cool to play a normal mom. I wasn't playing the sex symbol." She adds that it was only through Peaches's personal friendship, which fostered awareness of her as more than only Elvira, that her casting was possible, saying, "I would have never been cast by anyone else, not by anyone in the world, except a friend who knew me." *Midnight Mass*, episode 14.

37. In my 2017 interview, Peaches said, "I always saw Steven as young Peaches."

38. Joshua Grannell (Peaches Christ) in conversation with the author, August 26, 2017.

—ɯ—

WHY DO WE GO INTO THE WOODS?

AT THE TIME OF WRITING, it is May 2022. Recently, Florida passed the Parental Rights in Education bill, popularly called the "Don't Say Gay" bill, which strictly censors discussion of queer topics in Florida's public schools with little guidance as to what may or may not make school districts liable to lawsuits by parents who feel the curriculum is age inappropriate. On Twitter, Christina Pushaw, the press secretary for Florida governor Ron DeSantis, stated that if you oppose the bill "you are probably a groomer," invoking fears of child sexual abuse by queer educators not unlike those stoked by Anita Bryant and Save Our Children in the 1970s.[1] We are still amid the era of arguing for "parental rights" as antidote to advancements in queer civil rights. Soon after, Alabama passed legislation banning gender affirming healthcare for children and prohibiting trans children from using their correct bathrooms in schools, to which they added additional language mirroring the Florida bill's prevention of curriculum discussing gender identity and sexual orientation.[2] Florida and Texas have similarly conveyed guidance against gender affirming care for children, which has left healthcare providers unsure of if and how they might proceed in the future.[3] Just this week, *Politico* published a leaked draft of a US Supreme Court decision that suggests the court has voted to overturn the ruling of *Roe v. Wade*, the landmark 1973 decision that affirmed the right to medical privacy regarding pregnancy prior to twenty-two weeks and created federal protection in the United States for abortions and other reproductive healthcare.[4] The language of the decision, not yet law, suggests the court may begin to erode the interpretation of the "unenumerated" right to privacy in the 14th Amendment of the US Constitution, on which Roe was founded. We are left to wonder if in the future we might face further challenges to other precedent-setting court cases about reproductive healthcare and queer sexuality whose decisions were also based on the right to privacy, namely 1965's *Griswold v. Connecticut* (affirming the right to contraception) and 2003's *Lawrence v. Texas* (which made state antisodomy laws unenforceable).[5] For the past semester, teaching Intro to Queer Studies has required weekly updates about landmark civil rights advancements that have again come under fire. I'm not having a great day.

Thus far in this book, I have looked at how queer slashers might reformulate the subgenre to name our abusers and destigmatize queer positions (*Serial Mom*) or explore a conflicted position of spectatorship for queer viewers within an ideology of heteronormativity (*All About Evil*). In this final chapter, I want to look at one of the most difficult questions we face when dealing with queer slashers: the question of mediated violence by queer characters and against queer characters. Those slashers where we watch a group of queer friends picked off one at a time by a queer killer. Where there is no displacement or disavowal of the queerness in the violence and victimization at play. To do this, I want to look at one of the most nuanced and beautiful films of this kind, *Stranger by the Lake* (Alain Guiraudie, 2013). Given the current political difficulties queer people are facing in state legislation and owing to a majority conservative Supreme Court, I am inspired more than ever to consider the vital function of a film that confesses rather than denies the ongoing feelings of dread and despair often associated with being a queer person.

Stranger by the Lake takes place exclusively at a gay cruising beach in France. The protagonist, Franck (Pierre Deladonchamps), is a regular at the beach. We see him develop two integral relationships over the course of the film. The first is a nonsexual connection with Henri (Patrick d'Assumçao), a newcomer to the beach who has recently broken up with a girlfriend. Henri describes having previously spent time on "the other side" of the lake, where families go. Despite the cruising beach's social acceptance of nudity, Henri sits off to the side in his shorts, striking up conversations with Franck each day. He comments often about his fear of the silurus, a dangerously large species of catfish that is said to be found in the water. The second relationship is with Michel (Christophe Paou), the prized stud of the beach to whom Franck is very attracted. One night, Michel drowns his lover Pascal (François-Renaud Labarthe) in the lake, and Franck witnesses the fatal attack. Despite knowing Michel is a murderer, Franck remains infatuated with him, and the two begin a sexual relationship. Franck alludes often to wishing they could meet somewhere away from the beach, but Michel adamantly restricts their relationship to this one spot. When the body of Pascal is discovered, Inspector Damroder (Jérôme Chappatte) arrives to investigate. He interrogates the cruising community about both the murder and their collective way of life. Though the inspector suspects Michel is involved, Franck denies knowing anything several times. In a climactic scene, Henri confronts Michel about whether Franck will meet the same fate as Pascal. Henri then enters the nearby woods, the part of the cruising area where sex most frequently occurs. He is followed by Michel. Franck later discovers Henri's bleeding body in the woods. Then Franck observes Michel stab Inspector Damroder. Franck hides among the bushes as Michel requests that he show himself. Eventually, Franck steps out into the darkness and calls Michel's name.

On the surface, *Stranger by the Lake* may appear anomalous, or at least differentiated, when compared to the films discussed in the two prior chapters. Namely because it is the only one of the three produced outside the United States (it was made in the south of France). It's also the least predictably adherent to the slasher's pattern of sequential kills, particularly stabbing murders. The film has only a few sparse deaths, and only two are stabbings (one of which is off screen). As I disclosed in the introduction to this book, I see the category of the slasher as it exists in scholarship and popular culture as a tool to think about and better understand media. I am not motivated to make an essentializing case that *Stranger by the Lake* is or is not categorically a slasher. Recalling Eve Sedgwick's concept of universalizing and minoritizing discourses that eschews simple binaries, we might think of genre as both a distinct set of films that adhere reliably to genre traits and a flexible umbrella under which many titles might be considered to raise questions about their function and place in the cinematic landscape. There are no doubt other cinematic traditions intersecting in the makeup of *Stranger by the Lake*, including those of French cinema and queer erotica. However, it seems to me that the slasher might also be one meaningful way to think about *Stranger by the Lake*.

Among those qualities that the slasher helps us better understand in this film and that, additionally, this film helps us better understand about the modern queer slasher are its uses of sexual voyeurism and sexualized violence. Throughout this chapter, I will argue that *Stranger by the Lake* makes notable changes to how these tropes are utilized and that these alterations open up exciting queer meanings. To begin, *Stranger by the Lake* presents the disruption of a picturesque landscape in a way that recalls the slasher's own problematizing of an idyllic tableau, albeit a French gay cruising beach rather than a US suburb. Adam Lowenstein observes in his study of what he calls "subtractive spectatorship" that the serial "subtraction" of characters by the killer in both the slasher and Italian giallo brings us closer to the bare natural landscape.[6] Lowenstein expresses the appeal of "subtractive spectatorship" through discussion of Freud's theory of the "death drive," meaning that these films explore a pleasure in seeing the natural landscape emptied of humanity and a collective return to the natural world. *Stranger by the Lake* plays on both the appeal of fatality, the allure of an erotic flirtation with death, and the subtraction (by murder) of bodies from its beach. Notably, this appeal of subtraction is amplified here by the queer sexual politics of safe sex and the antiqueer rhetoric spurred by the AIDS crisis, as I will discuss later.

The film also echoes the slasher's common invocation of myth in both setting and character archetype. Vera Dika describes the fictional setting of Haddonfield in *Halloween* (John Carpenter, 1978) as defined by its nondescript American middle-class normalcy without a specific visual designation of time or place in its design. She calls it "Anytown U.S.A." and "a paradigmatic, almost mythic representation."[7] She also observes that by taking place on a recurring holiday, the film "introduces a theme of cycles, or repetitions" rather than merely finite periodization.[8] *Stranger by the Lake* director Alain Guiraudie likewise reflects on his movie's enmeshed temporality, identifying how "the film really takes place now, but, as in pretty much all of my films, there's always a mixture of the present and the 1970s."[9] He further speaks of the film's repetitious restaging of the lake's daily activities as "mythification" and expresses a desire to "make the everyday seem more mythical."[10] The mythic also manifests in the film's use of identifiable archetypes. Previously, I have discussed how the archetypes of heteronormative teenagers, so undistinguished and ordinary as to seem like a cross section of appealing commercial norms, populate the classical slasher and how queer slashers invoke their own archetypes such as the TV mom (*Serial Mom*) and the bad moviegoer (*All About Evil*) to stand in for a cultural idea. Alain Giraudie describes the casting process for Christophe Paou as one that helped him reimagine the character of Michel as a "gay icon," meaning more of an imagined gay ideal of masculinity than a realistic depiction of a man. He states, "Michel got taken closer toward being a gay icon in the manner of Freddie Mercury or Tom Selleck. He could come out of an album by Tom of Finland."[11] These remarks merge the mythic temporality of *Stranger by the Lake*, referring to Michel as someone akin to a 1970s sex symbol while also engaging with the idea of Michel as an archetypal dreamboat. The kind of man gay artists have drawn as their fantasy in erotica. As if he emerged from the screen or the printed page.

To understand how *Stranger by the Lake* meaningfully varies the slasher's common form, I would like to consider the idea of a queer counterpublic and particularly how the sexual politics of the gay cruising beach necessitate changes to the slasher's conventions due to the altered relationship between sex and violence in this space. In "Sex in Public," Lauren Berlant and Michael Warner argue that sex and intimacy have been made private in favor of a public sphere that segregates "true personhood" from "citizens, workers, or professionals."[12] That heterosexuality is structurally reinforced through aspects of public life in the form of marriage, family law, joint bank accounts, etc. and legislators leverage this invisible pervasiveness to sustain the idea that sexuality and intimacy are private. Queer communities, however, become burdened with the perception that their sex is foregrounded by their very existence. The communities themselves thereby violate the logic that sex should be private because they are viewed as innately and flagrantly, if not criminally, sexual. Berlant and Warner offer the example that legislation dislocating erotic bookstores from their queer communities due to standards mandating distance from certain community buildings such as churches or schools effectively destroys the queer community built upon this base level of sexual commerce. They argue that these erotic spaces create places for queer people to meet and cruise and that it is upon this sexual community that social spaces such as coffee shops and performance venues are often built. By eradicating sex from the public sphere, heteronormativity maintains its visual dominance while effectively stymying the development of a queer world.

According to Berlant and Warner, a queer counterpublic is an opportunity for queer culture to exist through "nonstandard intimacies" that create "a public world of belonging and transformation."[13] Such a space evades the notion that the intimate and the sexual should be private and instead creates new forms of public and communal intimacy wherein sex can be a part of public life. Importantly, this does not entail the re-creation of heteronormative relationships among queer individuals but instead provides a complete retooling of intimate relations toward queer aims. Berlant and Warner state that "making a queer world has required the development of kinds of intimacy that bear no necessary relation to domestic space, to kinship, to the couple form, to property, or to the nation" but that these intimacies instead "bear a necessary relation to a counterpublic—an indefinitely accessible world conscious of its subordinate relation."[14]

I would like to think of the gay cruising beach of *Stranger by the Lake* as one such queer counterpublic, a space in which a queer world of intimacies forms that is subordinate to the heteronormative community on "the other side" of the lake, where the families go. One totally apart from heteronormative society, separate from work, country, or kin. It is an overt feature of *Stranger by the Lake* that we never leave the space of the beach. The film reimagines the slasher as it might exist in this queer counterpublic that refigures public relations. One of the slasher's historically prominent features has been its setting in the predominantly white middle-class suburbs. In chapter 1, I discussed how the slasher can be said to visualize a collision between a queer outsider (the killer) and white bourgeois heteronormative society and how the killer's assault on this picturesque assemblage of norms could be seen as an attack on heteronormativity itself. This construction cannot be said to carry through to *Stranger by the Lake* as heteronormative communities do not play a role, and the setting is instead made into an exclusively queer, albeit still overwhelmingly white, space. It is a slasher set within a queer community, in which we are both killer and victim. The shift in setting heavily problematizes a thesis of the slasher as an attack on heteronormativity and prompts a reexamination of how this queer slasher explores sex and violence in and among queer communities.

Canonical slashers of the 1970s and '80s are commonly perceived as reactionary films that punish women for their liberated sexuality. In popular culture, we see this idea espoused clearly in the special 1980 episode of Siskel and Ebert's review show *Sneak Previews* titled "Women In Danger," which criticized recent films such as *Friday the 13th* (Sean S. Cunningham, 1980) and *The Silent Scream* (Denny Harris, 1979).[15] In scholarship, this idea is expressed most clearly by Robin Wood in his articulation of what he calls the "teenie-kill pic" (which loosely describes several teen-targeted slashers of the 1970s and '80s) and the "violence against women movie" (reserved more for adult fare like Brian De Palma's 1980 thriller *Dressed to Kill*). According to Wood, the main difference between the categories is the motive for punishment on the part of the killer. "In general," he states, "the teenagers are punished for promiscuity, while the women are punished for being women."[16] While I have argued for a different engagement with the slasher's violence in this book, I would never suggest films work in only one way or have just one meaning. In chapter 4, I tried to wrestle with the complex position of spectatorship as a queer fan of slashers who acknowledges their misogynist violence and homophobic/transphobic use of queer killers while also working through a persistent affectionate attachment. What interests me about these critical characterizations of the slasher is how they speak to a wider narrative of these films understood even by casual moviegoers. So much so that in Kevin Williamson's screenplay for *Scream* (Wes Craven, 1996), Randy (Jamie Kennedy) openly admonishes a room full of teen partygoers that they must remain virgins if they wish to survive.

The popularly quoted formula that sex equals death provides context for how sex and violence are seen to work in tandem during 1970s and '80s slashers. It has been argued that the violence of the slasher is itself a deferred sexual assault. Carol J. Clover states that "actual rape is practically nonexistent in the slasher film, evidently on the premise . . . that violence and sex are not concomitants but alternatives."[17] Discussing *The Texas Chain Saw Massacre* (Tobe Hooper, 1974), Robin Wood makes the case that sexual impulses are sublimated into violence. He writes, "Here sexuality is totally perverted from its functions into sadism, violence, and cannibalism. It is striking that no suggestion exists anywhere that Sally is the object of an overtly sexual threat: she is to be tormented, killed, dismembered, eaten, but not raped."[18] The killer may be read here as a stand-in for a sexually frustrated heterosexual predator, but I would also situate this within a broader queer history (discussed in chap. 1) of the eroticized look of the killer leading to a form of physical assault that highlights his failure to participate in heterosexuality. Killers with queer traits such as those in *The Lodger* (John Brahm, 1944), *The Spiral Staircase* (Robert Siodmak, 1946), and *Psycho* (Alfred Hitchcock, 1960) whose voyeurism results in murder, not sexual assault.

This legacy leads to the common assertion of a pattern in the slasher where women are stalked and then killed, often with a knife or other weapon with a sexual connotation, though the attack itself is not commonly sexual. It is also what shapes the belief that it is the sexually liberated teens, the nonvirgins, who "get it" in the end. Drawing on Berlant and Warner, it may be said that the slasher reflects heteronormative society's project of private sexuality. Sex is sought after by teens in private bedrooms and in stolen moments of isolation that make them vulnerable to the killer's knife. Teens who pair off out of sight for sex are notoriously signaled as soon-to-be victims in part because of their choice to enter arrangements of private intimacy that seclude them from the group and any larger community. By shifting locations from the heteronormative suburbs to the queer counterpublic of the gay cruising beach, *Stranger by the Lake* also alters the relationship between sex and violence. Sex on the cruising beach is public and plentiful. It is surveilled consistently by voyeurs and masturbators who like to watch. In an early scene, Franck's sex partner of the moment asks if he minds the masturbator who watches them from the bushes, to which Franck responds indifferently that if it makes him happy, why not? This type of reformatted public intimacy that takes part within the larger group also undoes much of the classic formulation of the slasher as the teens who separate for sex and become victims are not a part of this film's motifs.

In fact, *Stranger by the Lake* depicts sex as omnipresent and perfunctory to the point that it almost becomes banal. It is not a special event, a moment of taboo allure or titillation as seen in the canonical slasher. It is everywhere all the time. The men on the beach, save for Henri, are almost always nude, with their penises in clear view of the camera even in moments of casual dialogue. There is no erotic buildup to a reveal of the naked body. Instead, it is a kind of daily routine. One pulls up to the beach, spreads a towel, and reveals one's body to the group and to the camera. The habitual nature of the beach is emphasized by a reoccurring, static establishing shot of the parking lot that shows cars arriving each day, repeatedly and reliably, the same as the day before. In addition to the consistent nudity, sex in the film is highly visible and not especially limited in how it is portrayed. This is made most apparent by the film's choice to feature unsimulated sex acts, including an on-screen ejaculation and a scene of fellatio. In a movie where cock sucking and jizz-shooting dicks are found in plain sight, what, then, is a killer to do? I argue that while

You don't mind being watched?

Fig 5.1 Sex in plain sight. An anonymous lover asks Franck if he minds the masturbator watching them have sex in the woods in *Stranger by the Lake* (2013).

the canonical slasher sublimates sex into its violence, fueling the killer's murder spree with a phallic connotation in the form of the knife, in *Stranger by the Lake* the inverse is true: violence is sublimated into sex. In the queer counterpublic of the cruising beach, sex is essential to the fabric of public life. Conversely, it is violence that offers a taboo allure, and arguably it is what Franck seeks but always misses when pursuing sex with Michel. To loosely rewrite Carol J. Clover's assertion that "slasher killers are by generic definition sexually inadequate—men who kill precisely because they cannot fuck," I would offer that in *Stranger by the Lake* men fuck because they cannot kill (or be killed).[19] Or at the very least, the potential for violence is what fuels much of the central eroticism of the relationship between Franck and Michel. And while sex is apparent and abundant (rather than restricted from view or reserved for private moments), violence is rare and maintains a complex appeal.

The film underscores this in the scenes leading up to and including the murder of Michel's lover, Pascal. In the scene that precedes the murder, Franck enters the woods with another man (Gilbert Traina, credited only as "Tuesday night man"). The two men initiate sex but then stop. The partner complains about the onlooking masturbator, which Franck shrugs off. Franck then

attempts to perform fellatio, which the partner rebuffs, asking
if Franck has a condom. Franck is turned off by the request. It
turns out neither of them has one. The two bicker a bit about
what to do next. A cut suggests the passing of time. Franck is now
masturbating and asks the partner to kiss him while he orgasms.
We see a close-up of Franck's hand stroking his erect penis as
he ejaculates. Franck then places his partner's hand around his
penis. The partner grips him firmly. The two men continue to
kiss. This is arguably the most public and visible sexual moment
of the film. It represents the most restricted of sexual attributes
on film, an erect penis ejaculating, in close-up and in broad daylight as an unsimulated sex act open to the visual inspection of
aroused onlookers. It is sharply juxtaposed against the following
scene in which Michel murders Pascal. Unlike the clear close-up
of Franck's orgasm, this scene takes place at night, in darkness.
The camera's vantage point of the lake is from deep in the woods,
where Franck voyeuristically observes the two men swimming.
The view is obscured by tree branches and foliage in the foreground. At first, it is not at all clear what we are seeing or where
in the frame we should look to locate the source of the sounds
we hear: splashing and laughing. We assume, as Franck probably
does, that we are stumbling onto a sexual liaison as with all the
other beach scenes in the film. We finally see the pair at the cen-
ter of the frame, but in an extreme long shot that keeps Franck's
distant position in the woods. The two are splashing and dunk-
ing each other's heads beneath the water in a way that appears to
be playful. It is not entirely clear when and how the mood turns.
The laughter becomes pleading. We see one man force the other's
head below the water and not allow him to return to the surface.
The surviving man swims to shore, toward the camera. As he gets
closer, the camera pushes in on him. When he emerges, we (and
Franck) see it is Michel.

Franck's sexual relationship with Michel begins in the wake
of his discovery that Michel is a murderer. It is innately charged

with the threat of Michel's violence and perhaps intensified because of it. Their first sexual encounter plays as something like an
inverse of the earlier unsatisfying encounter with the condom-
preferring man in the woods. Michel makes immediate advances
to perform fellatio on Franck with no request for a condom. In a
later conversation, Franck will specifically ask Michel if he can
fuck him without a condom, and Michel will gladly agree. Unlike
the highly safe sexual encounter that preceded the murder, this
one is dangerous both because it is unprotected (condomless)
sex and because it is sex with a murderer. Franck's orgasm during his first sexual encounter with Michel mirrors the previous
ejaculation scene but with several meaningful differences. While
the earlier one was brightly lit and set in broad daylight, Franck's
first orgasm with Michel is staged at night. Their bodies are un-
derlit in the foreground, which causes them to appear as solid
black silhouettes cast against the backdrop of the lake, a constant visual reminder of Michel's murder. Franck has knowingly
agreed to stay alone with Michel into the night, putting himself
in jeopardy of the same fate. As before, Franck masturbates and
asks Michel to kiss him as he orgasms. They are two dark silhouettes set before the glimmering lake. There is no close-up or
clear visualization of Franck's orgasm. It is as if with the added
danger of physical violence, the sex is suddenly more illicit, less
visible to the camera's eye, altogether less ordinary and mundane. As the two exit the beach, Michel asks about Franck's car,
which, he remarks, is unique as they are no longer manufactured.
This strongly intimates that Michel would have noticed Franck's
unique car, which was the only car left in the parking lot on the
evening of the murder besides that of the victim. This increases
the threat of violence around their relationship as we wonder
what Michel might do with this information or whether this was
the reason for his pursual of Franck in the first place.

As a queer slasher, *Stranger by the Lake* dramatizes the complicated allure that self-destructive sexual behaviors can have

Fig 5.2 Franck and Michel have sex alone on the beach at night in *Stranger by the Lake* (2013). They are inky-black silhouettes set before the lake where Michel murdered his lover, Pascal.

within queer communities. However, unlike classical slashers set in the heteronormative suburbs, the queerness of the killer here is not a novel quality that positions him as an outsider. The queer counterpublic of the beach is a space upon which a thriving community is built outside of heteronormative society. It is by no means utopian, but it is a space of relative freedom wherein queer intimacies can be formed as part of public life. Much of the sex that happens there is safe. Most of its regulars are of no harm. Queer sexualities themselves are not universally implicated as dangerous behavior. However, the film acknowledges that for some there is an appeal to danger. It parallels Franck's interest in murderer Michel with his request for condomless sex, which seemingly nods to an accepted risk of HIV or other STIs. I don't wish to read *Stranger by the Lake* as HIV allegory but instead fold in this detail among others that address a spectrum of self-endangering practices Franck undertakes in his sexual relationship with Michel.

One way the lessons of the AIDS crisis can help us understand the experience that Franck seeks out is found in Leo Bersani's 1987 essay "Is the Rectum a Grave?" which poses integral questions about perceptions of danger within queer sexualities, particularly anal sex among men. Reflecting on media discourse of the 1980s, Bersani observes a pattern of associating queer men with promiscuity, which in turn brands them as conveyors of disease and ultimately killers. He connects this observation to a history that characterized women sex workers in the nineteenth century as open carriers of syphilis. He explains that both '80s AIDS and nineteenth-century syphilis discourse legitimate a fantasy of women's sexuality as "intrinsically diseased" and of sexual promiscuity as not merely a risk but a "sign of infection."[20] It is this perception of gay men in the '80s as diseased killers that he says motivates the violent animosity against them. He situates this within the larger moral taboo of men acting in "passive" sex roles, observing that historically "to be penetrated is to abdicate power" and therefore an affront to a phallocentric society that devalues powerlessness.[21] Bersani takes up the "appeal of powerlessness" and argues that sex should be about "the radical disintegration and humiliation of the self."[22] Drawing on Freud, he develops the idea of sex as "ecstatic suffering" or "self-shattering" in which pain and pleasure blur.[23] The active, insertive sex role in this formulation, he says, "inaccurately mistakes self-shattering as self-swelling, as psychic tumescence," asserting the ego rather than shattering it."[24] Bersani urges readers to instead embrace passive, receptive sex roles as demeaning, as shattering the phallocentric ego rather than reinforcing it. He concludes, "If the rectum is the grave in which the masculine ideal . . . of proud subjectivity is buried, then it should be celebrated for its very potential for death."[25] And that the value of queer sex among men is how "it never stops re-presenting the internalized phallic male as an infinitely loved object of sacrifice."[26]

Bersani's theory about the value of powerlessness and his characterization of receptive queer sex as a ritual of sacrificing the phallic male ego informs my understanding of Franck's path away from the counterpublic of the beach and toward sex that always carries the risk of death. In a sense, we can understand Franck's journey as one that is persistently testing limits, infinitely placing himself in a position of powerlessness that inches ever closer to the complete loss of self, to a literal death whose appeal tempts him but that is, in the meantime, sated by an ongoing sexual relationship with Michel in which his urge toward powerlessness and self-debasement becomes eroticized and persistently renewed. Their relationship entails a series of recommitments to the circumstance of Franck's vulnerability to violence. We can see this in his choice to pursue Michel, to stay alone with him at night, to accept the intimation about the car, to deny any knowledge of the murder to the inspector, and lastly as he steps out into the dark and calls Michel's name in the film's finale. In one especially suspenseful scene set at dusk, Michel and Franck lie alone on the beach. Michel decides to swim in the lake and asks Franck to join him. Franck declines at first, citing the fact that someone just died in the lake. Michel swims out alone. Franck concedes and follows him anyway. Away from shore, Franck's eyes dart around the empty lake as Michel swims toward him. The scene heavily emphasizes Franck's choice to re-create the scenario of Pascal's murder. Michel arrives near him, and the two kiss. They briefly dip below the water but then resurface. They smile and laugh. We cut to a long shot of them that is nearly identical to the earlier shot of Michel and Pascal just before the murder, acknowledging the symmetry between scenes. We then smash cut to Franck and Michel fucking on the beach. The scene suggests Franck's choice to court death was a form of foreplay.

In addition to this isolated and dangerous sexuality with Michel, Franck also spends the film exploring a second figure of interest: Henri. Michel and Henri represent decidedly different appeals. While Michel offers a self-debasing and highly erotic private sexuality outside of the social beach routine, Henri sits to the side of the beach as something of an inactive interloper. He is always dressed, never nude, and never seen to be a part of the sexual public of the beach, not even as an erotic voyeur.

Fig 5.3 Franck wades into the lake alone with Michel, willfully choosing to re-create the circumstances of Pascal's murder.

He is associated with family and the couple form through his references to a recent breakup with a girlfriend and previous experience on "the other side" of the lake where families go. He is also the only one of the beachgoers associated with work as he discloses that he is a logger enjoying a three-week holiday. When Franck approaches Henri in his secluded place to the side of the cruising beach, Henri remarks that Franck should cover himself because nudity is not allowed on this part of the beach. Franck remarks that it is not technically "allowed" (presumably, in a legal sense) on the cruising beach either but is socially accepted. Henri and Franck discuss having been to dinner together and sharing meetings outside of the beach area (which we never see). However, they definitively acknowledge they are not interested in sex together. This is highly contrary to Franck's connection with Michel, which exclusively takes place at the beach, significantly at night when the crowd is gone. Franck repeatedly suggests he and Michel meet elsewhere at night, for dinner or other social plans, but Michel adamantly refuses a relationship outside of this space and beyond the realm of the sexual.

To understand how Bersani and Berlant/Warner's frameworks help to explain the dramatization of queer relationships in *Stranger by the Lake*, it is relevant to take note of what they express their concepts as excluding or working against. Namely that Bersani's theory of sex as the "disintegration and humiliation of the self" is argued as an alternative to circulating ideas of the period that he alleges idealize gay bathhouses and other cruising spaces by rewriting a degrading space into a utopian queer enclave of sexual community.[27] He counters instead that the value for such a space is in its humiliation and its ability to demean the phallic ego. Berlant and Warner, in "Sex in Public," assert that a counterpublic must be forged through nonstandard intimacies and not by re-creating versions of heteronormative relations. They argue that queer people accomplish the latter "only by betrothing themselves to the couple form and its language of personal significance, leaving untransformed the material and ideological conditions that divide intimacy from history, politics, and publics."[28] We can use Bersani's theory of valuably demeaning sexuality to help understand one path that lures Franck away from the sexual public of the beach via Michel. Further still, we can utilize Berlant/Warner's distinction between a counterpublic and queer relations that reproduce the values of heteronormativity to understand Franck's other alluring pull away from the beach community via Henri, whose relationship with Franck complies with narratives of the domestic couple in a same-sex combination. Henri signals a pull toward "the other side" of the lake but also to a world beyond the sexual public of the beach and toward a sentimentality that reaffirms the construction of intimacy as private and separate from the public sphere.

Lisa Duggan has characterized this potential for a new form of queer relationship that reaffirms the values of heteronormativity as "homonormativity." She describes homonormativity as "a politics that does not contest dominant heteronormative assumptions and institutions, but upholds and sustains them, while promising the possibility of a demobilized gay constituency and a privatized, depoliticized gay culture anchored in domesticity and consumption."[29] This neoliberal "equality politics" severs affiliations with the progressive left and instead advocates for gay "normality." She describes this as a corporation-driven politics that serves "an increasingly narrow gay, moneyed elite" by eschewing an intersectional progressive queer movement and focusing instead on highly limited legislative issues such as gay marriage and military service.[30] Activists of this movement work to forge an alleged "gay mainstream," marketing this as a "third way" positioned against both queer progressivism and antigay conservatism. To do this, they engage in what Duggan calls "a rhetorical restructuring of public/private boundaries designed to shrink gay public spheres, and redefine gay equality against the 'civil rights agenda' and 'liberationism,' as access to the institutions of domestic privacy, the 'free' market, and patriotism."[31] The creation and preservation of gay publics, Duggan argues, has been an essential project of the gay movement. What she calls the right to "privacy-in-public" was a central aim of the 1950s homophile movement, which sought to protect gays and lesbians from government surveillance and harassment. This included addressing discrimination by police, state liquor authorities, and the FBI in bars, cruising parks, and workplaces with the intention to "expand the allowable scope of sexual expression in public culture."[32] Gay liberation of the 1970s further sought public visibility for gays and lesbians, "a right to publicize 'private' matters considered offensive to the phantom 'general public.'"[33] However, by the '80s, antigay movements had shifted their argument away from the outright criminalization of queer sexuality and toward a mission to enforce the idea that these relations ought to be "private." This led to attacks on federal funding of queer art and pushback against the gay movement's aim to politicize the private. Critics argued queer sexualities should be isolated to private, domestic spheres and not "promoted." The AIDS crisis also created new forms of gay moralism advocating monogamy and antipromiscuity as disease-control methodologies. Duggan argues that since the '90s, strains of this moralism critiquing the

"gay lifestyle" have led to the creation of a gay politics, primarily adopted among wealthy white men, that aims to narrow gay
publics and focus solely on select legislative issues relevant to
them while also depoliticizing the position of gays and lesbians
by making sexuality a "private" domestic issue.

In a big picture sense, it's not especially important to align
the film's characters and settings singularly with these different
threads within queer theory and politics. However, I am com-
pelled by the idea that what *Stranger by the Lake* achieves as a
queer slasher is a more complex exploration of the queer subject
position for white gay men, especially at a moment of more political openness toward ideas of homonormativity and marriage
equality. *Obergefell v. Hodges* protected marriage equality at the
federal level in the United States in 2015, just a few years after
the film's release, while France passed a bill legalizing same-sex
marriage that became law on May 18, 2013, coincidentally just one
day after *Stranger by the Lake* premiered at the Cannes Film Festi-
val. Where I have argued the canonical slasher cycle of the 1970s
and '80s captured a rebellious energy of queer resistance toward
white bourgeois heteronormativity found in the initial mission
statements of gay liberation activist groups, *Stranger by the Lake*
complicates this narrative with multiple possibilities available for
Franck. This allows the film to explore with greater nuance how
the gay movement in all its forms was never singular nor wholly
unified and that gay white men have long been tempted into positions that nullify the movement's revolutionary potential in favor
of positions within the heteronormative regime. Franck is presented with three options: (1) to conform to the homonormative
couple that depoliticizes gay sexuality and limits it to private domesticity, (2) to forge a new sexual counterpublic of nonstandard
queer intimacies, or (3) to make an antisocial turn away from
public life through habitual explorations of sexual powerlessness.

The contentious divisions of the gay liberation movement
of the 1970s can be seen in emblematic moments such as trans

activist Sylvia Rivera's emotional speech at the 1973 Christopher Street Liberation Day celebration in New York City's Washington Square Park commemorating the fourth anniversary of the Stonewall riots. Often colloquially referred to as "Y'all Better Quiet Down" in reference to the first phrase spoken by Rivera toward the hostile, booing crowd. Rivera's remarks indicted white middle-class gays and lesbians for their failure to protect trans individuals, especially trans people of color, and to acknowledge the plight of the incarcerated. Rivera, along with Marsha P. Johnson, formed STAR (Street Transvestite Action Revolutionaries) to help support and house trans individuals facing the worst forms of public harassment and police violence due to their public gender nonconforming expressions. In interviews, Rivera commented on disrespect she faced from cis gay men in mainstream groups like GAA (Gay Activists Alliance), describing their refusal to use her correct name as well as continued references to her as a "drag queen" despite objections.[34] Similarly, groups like Combahee River Collective formed in response to the failure of the mainstream gay liberation movement to address the needs of Black lesbians. In their initial mission statement, Combahee River Collective outlined their theory of interlocking oppressions, drawing on their overlapping experiences of racial, sexual, heterosexual, and class oppression. They theorized that a politics of Black feminism was inherently a politics of universal liberation because "if Black women were free, it would mean that everyone else would have to be free since our freedom would necessitate the destruction of all the systems of oppression."[35]

As I work on revisions to this manuscript, it is now May 2023. Almost one whole year since the US Supreme Court decision that loomed over the beginning of this chapter. In that time, the underlying implications about the ruling's suggestion of an undue constitutional right to medical privacy have no doubt contributed to a massive rise in state legislation intervening into the medical care of trans individuals, especially trans children. States such

as Tennessee, Florida, and Montana have passed legislation banning gender affirming care for minors.[36] This marks an outright
invasion by the government into private conversations about
medical care. It's also a further indication of the increased vulnerability of trans communities relative to their cisgender queer
peers. While private decisions with medical providers are being
made into public legislative issues, queer and trans expressions
in public are again facing erasure against a rhetoric that deems all
public queerness innately sexual and harmful to minors. This can
be seen in laws passed in Tennessee and Montana that expressly
prohibit drag performances in places where minors are present.
The rhetoric around this legislation continues a now decades-old
tradition of insinuating that queers are pedophiles and that drag
shows innately sexualize children, which they do not. These laws
also indirectly endanger trans individuals as their language gives
no clear indication of what constitutes drag relative to trans identity. In my deepest fears, I worry we may backslide into a reality
not unlike the conditions pre-Stonewall in which public displays
of queer identity, especially gender nonconforming and trans expressions, are themselves deemed perverse, innately sexual, and
illegal. The conversations in this chapter regarding the limiting
of queerness in public and the political potential for creating a
queer counterpublic on the foundations of bodily autonomy and
sexual freedom are even more pertinent. However, so too is the
looming sense of dread that fuels the appeal of self-annihilation.
A wish to vanish into the lake, as it were.

Stranger by the Lake explores the appeal of self-annihilation during its finale, in which Henri, almost suicidally, accuses Michel of
murder and then goes into the woods alone, choosing vulnerability in much the way Franck has throughout the film. This entails
Henri exiting his position in limbo between the two sides of the
lake and firmly entering the gay cruising side for the first time. He
sits beside Michel on the beach and confronts him about his murder of Pascal and likely threat to Franck. Then Henri announces

he will go for a walk in the woods. As he reaches the threshold, he turns back to look at Michel as if beckoning him to follow, cruising to be killed. When Franck approaches, an eye-line match establishes that he sees Michel moving around atop a body behind some foliage. A nonverbal vocalization is heard. The scene recalls Michel's murder of Pascal, again emphasizing an overlap in sights and sounds where sex and murder are not entirely discernible from each other. When Michel emerges, Franck gets closer and sees Henri on the ground with his throat slit. In his final moments, Henri discourages Franck from trying to save him and states that he got what he was after. We are left, as is Franck, wondering about Henri's decision to surrender to Michel in the woods. Having never stripped or cruised at the beach or even entered the cruising area, the gesture seems like a sharp traversal across a spatial and political divide. We are left to wonder if Henri's fraught position physically between the two sides of the beach and politically between heteronormativity and a queer community left him feeling hopeless, as if his conflicted existence would be impossible to sustain. Or if there was an element of erotic pleasure sought in the violence that was fulfilled by his murder.

Franck's repeated choice of sex with Michel simulates his own inevitable demise at Michel's hands. Their relationship appears sustained by an erotic tension built around the potential to reach not a sexual but a murderous climax, a release that sex seems to temporarily defer by diverting violent energies into more palatable and readily available sex acts. We see this when Franck offers himself as a victim of murder by swimming out into the lake with Michel, who chooses instead to consummate the violent tension between them with sex on the beach. There is a potential to see Henri's choice to pursue a dangerous encounter with Michel along this same spectrum of testing limits and chasing violence that may end only in sex but could also end in death.

We are left without clear answers as to why Henri makes the choice to go with Michel into the woods or why Franck, seemingly still committed to his pursuit, steps into the open during the film's final frames and calls Michel's name. However, it seems fair to say that the film engages with the idea that submission to a powerless position can hold a spellbinding allure, perhaps especially among those imprinted with a sense of self-loathing by a heteronormative society that already conceives of their lives as perverse and destructive. Ultimately, this nihilism forms another of *Stranger by the Lake*'s notable departures from canonical slashers: its victims pursue their own demise, habitually and repeatedly. Unlike in a traditional slasher where scream queens attempt to run away and seek refuge from the killer in hopes of saving their lives, Franck keeps stepping into the fray, choosing Michel time after time in perilous circumstances that make him vulnerable to violence.

For me, the importance of *Stranger by the Lake* can best be understood through Heather Love's *Feeling Backward*, a study of negative texts in queer literature that outlines an important usefulness for these works in the larger queer political project. One salient point that Love makes is that queer politics are already phrased paradoxically through the discriminatory and medicalizing historical construction of queer identities. Building on Foucault, she notes the earliest precedent for homosexuality as reflecting personhood rather than behavior was in medical discourse that paved the way for homosexuality's historical perception as mental illness. The gay movement then sought to declare itself and pursue its visibility from within a conceptual framework established to classify them as a medical problem. Our affirmations of queer identities are always as backward looking as they are forward looking, reactively centered around a past of shame, stigma, and trauma. As Love states, "Pride and visibility offer antidotes to shame and the legacy of the closet; they are made in the image of specific forms of denigration."[37] For Love this reflects how queerness is both "abject and exalted," "a stigmatizing mark as well as a form of romantic exceptionalism." She argues this contrast becomes visible in the painful divide between progress/ acceptance oriented mainstream gay media and the lived realities of violence and discrimination queer people continue to face.[38] Love reflects on a conflicted relation to progress, expressing that a fallacy of continued gay historical progress across the twentieth century has been widely critiqued by queer theory. However, a belief in actual progress, a better world for queer people, is an essential part of a queer politics. She argues that critics are left struggling against a compulsion to inaccurately mend queer life in art. Negative texts that "underline the gap between aspiration and the actual" are often labeled "homophobic, retrograde, or too depressing to be of use."[39] Love contextualizes this within the move toward homonormativity, which makes narratives about shame and stigma less socially acceptable. The gay movement's turn toward isolated issues affecting a white middle class affords access to the mainstream for some gays and lesbians dependent upon their separation from those who cannot or do not conform for reasons pertaining to race, class, body type, gender identity, disability, or sexual activity. "Social negativity," she says, oppositely "clings not only to these figures but also to those who lived before the common era of gay liberation."[40] Where mainstream gay media advises us to forget our past and those in the present who are being left behind to seek a compromised place within heteronormativity, negative media allow us to continue to see ourselves in these experiences of denigration.

Stranger by the Lake is significant because it avoids any impulse to repair a queer history of the slasher. It does not diminish the queerness of the killer. In fact, it expands the slasher to include a full range of queer characters in an exclusively queer setting. It makes the slasher into a topography of the queer political intersection of mainstream assimilation, sexually liberated queer community, and the negative turn of submitting to danger. It further collapses our sense of distance from the past as the film is not clearly set in any one time. As Alain Guiraudie describes, the film is technically set in the present but stylistically invokes the 1970s. This achieves a form of mythic timelessness.[41] It is a gay cruising beach notably absent of cell phones and hookup apps. It sees gay cruising as an expansive practice taking place over decades of time and sets its characters in a space that appears to be at once both present and past. The discourse about condoms may feel, at first, to signal that we are watching a period film amid the AIDS crisis. Yet, the decision to never periodize the work sets the dialogue within a continuity that does not ask us to look back at a past world of dangerous cruising but instead signals the continuity of the issue of HIV/AIDS to generations of queer men up to and including the present. We are not allowed to only think "poor them" about queers in the past; instead, we are asked to see history as a throughline that envelops us. We are brought into the allure of sexual danger, which thwarts any possible contemporary position of judgment toward those living exterior to the modern moment of freer, safer queer lives. We are made to face that this danger has happened and still does happen. It is not "poor them." It's "poor us."

As a film, *Stranger by the Lake* embodies Franck's compulsive turn away a queer counterpublic toward the self-annihilating alure of Michel. It is a cinematic embrace of powerlessness, of choosing to go into the woods with a killer. It does not invite queer audiences to reshape their relation to the slasher's killer as in chapters 3 and 4 but instead to acknowledge the pain and burden of contemporary queer positions even among possibilities that suggest potential for equality or social progress. It encapsulates an experience wherein the overlapping and contrasting prospects of homonormative "equality" and reimagined queer communities might each, in their way, overlook or evade the undercurrent of danger to one's mental and physical health still present to this day. It invites us into the woods. Offers us an option to escape the narratives of progress undermined by daily experience. Gives us a chance to see our place in a long history of peril rather than subverting or rewriting the past. While much of this book has been about the queer slasher as a gesture toward a queer future created by the choice to step outside of "straight time" and imagine something that is not yet here, I would draw on Heather Love to offer that there is also within this framework a value in acknowledging rather than disavowing the painful realities of our present and past. *Stranger by the Lake* is a work that allows us to choose vulnerability and subject ourselves to trauma rather than only forging ahead in hope. It takes seriously the request for pain made tangible in pressing play or buying a ticket to a slasher movie. This transaction solidifies a choice made repeatedly by queer audiences to see cruel things happen to us on screen in ritualistic acknowledgment that they are still occurring in our world. We, as an audience, much like Franck, peruse the available cinematic options of the fun, sexy queer beach or the homonormative semi-mainstream and instead settle upon the macabre selection of the slasher, where we knowingly put ourselves in danger.

This is a book about how queer artists have taken a cinematic formula that implicates us in violence, the slasher, and created in its likeness a new canon of queer-made films that project onto it a hope for a cinema (and, therefore, a world) where we are seen (and see ourselves) differently. It is assuredly still that book. However, in this chapter I want to share the belief that to chart and stay any course of hope toward an always on the horizon future queer world, one might need to touch base with the present and the past, to know what has happened and feel its ramifications. Or else we run the risk of creating unsustainably forward-looking narratives that devalue the turn backward toward a bleak past that fuels the quest forward. A rest stop on the path to a plausible future, *Stranger by the Lake* lets us pause and assess where we have been, where we are, and why we need to get where we are going. It is grim and difficult, but it is part of a queer relation to the slasher that sees what it is and what it could be with an honesty that overlaps challenging pasts with potential futures. Why do we go into the woods? To see ourselves in the worn paths of generations past and to see our present in continuity with what has been and still could be.

NOTES

1. Brooke Migdon, "Gov. DeSantis Spokesperson Says 'Don't Say Gay' Opponents Are 'Groomers," *The Hill*, March 7, 2022, https://thehill.com /changing-america/respect/equality/597215-gov-desantis-spokesperson -says-dont-say-gay-opponents-are.

2. Brian Lyman, "Alabama Passes Expanded Version of Transgender 'Bathroom Bill' That Includes LGBTQ Discussion Ban," *USA Today*, April 8, 2022, https://www.usatoday.com/story/news/nation/2022/04/08 /alabama-dont-say-gay-bill/9510929002.

3. Anne Branigin, "Florida Memo on Gender Dysphoria Contradicts Leading Medical Guidance," *Washington Post*, April 20, 2022, https:// www.washingtonpost.com/politics/2022/04/20/florida-gender-dysphoria -memo; and Wade Goodwyn, "Texas Governor Calls to Label Gender-Affirming Care for Trans Kids as 'Child Abuse,'" *NPR*, March 1, 2022, https://www.npr.org/2022/03/01/1083775568/the-battle-around-medical -treatment-for-transgender-kids-in-texas-continues.

4. Josh Gerstein and Alexander Ward, "Supreme Court Has Voted to Overturn Abortion Rights, Draft Opinion," May 2, 2022, https://www .politico.com/news/2022/05/02/supreme-court-abortion-draft-opinion -00029473.

5. Milton J. Valencia, "With Roe Seemingly Undone, Other Rights Dating Back to Contraceptives Case Could Fall Under Attack," *Boston Globe*, May 14, 2022, https://www.bostonglobe.com/2022/05/14/metro /with-roe-seemingly-undone-other-rights-dating-back-contraceptives -case-could-fall-under-attack.

6. Lowenstein's theory of "subtractive spectatorship" is also explored in *Stranger by the Lake* in Elizabeth Erwin, "*Stranger by the Lake* and Subtractive Spectatorship," *Horror Homeroom*, August 22, 2020, https:// www.horrorhomeroom.com/stranger-by-the-lake-and-subtractive -spectatorship.

7. Vera Dika, *Games of Terror: Halloween, Friday the 13th, and the Films of the Stalker Cycle* (Madison, NJ: Farleigh Dickenson University Press, 1990), 35.

8. Dika, *Games of Terror*, 35.

9. R. Kurt Osenlund, "Interview: Alain Guiraudie on *Stranger by the Lake*," *Slant Magazine*, January 24, 2014, https://www.slantmagazine.com/film/interview-alain-guiraudie.

10. R. Kurt Osenlund, "Interview."

11. Alain Guiraudie, "Interview with Alain Guiraudie," *Stranger by the Lake*, DVD, directed by Alain Guiraudie (Culver City, CA: Strand Releasing, 2014).

12. Lauren Berlant and Michael Warner, "Sex in Public," *Critical Inquiry* 24, no. 2 (winter 1998): 559.

13. Berlant and Warner, "Sex in Public," 558–59.

14. Berlant and Warner, 558.

15. *Sneak Previews*, season 4, episode 4, "Women in Danger: Friday the 13th, Halloween, I Spit on Your Grave, Silent Scream, When a Stranger Calls, Don't Answer the Phone," directed by Dave Erdman, featuring Gene Siskel and Roger Ebert, aired September 18, 1980, on PBS.

16. Robin Wood, *Hollywood from Vietnam to Reagan* (New York: Columbia University Press, 1986), 195.

17. Carol J. Clover, *Men, Women, and Chain Saws: Gender in the Modern Horror Film* (Princeton, NJ: Princeton University Press, 1992), 29.

18. Wood, *Hollywood*, 91.

19. Clover, *Men, Women, and Chain Saws*, 186.

20. Leo Bersani, "Is the Rectum a Grave?," *October* 43 (winter 1987): 211.

21. Bersani, "Is the Rectum a Grave?," 212.

22. Bersani, 217.

23. Bersani, 217.

24. Bersani, 218.

25. Bersani, 222.

26. Bersani, 222.

27. Bersani, 205–07.

28. Berlant and Warner, "Sex in Public," 562.

29. Lisa Duggan, *The Twilight of Equality: Neoliberalism, Cultural Politics, and the Attack on Democracy* (Boston, MA: Beacon, 2003), 50.

30. Duggan, *The Twilight of Equality*, 45.

31. Duggan, 51.

32. Duggan, 52.

33. Duggan, 52–53.

34. Eric Marcus, "Bonus Episode—from the Vault: Sylvia Rivera & Marsha P. Johnson, 1970," December 27, 2019, *Making Gay History*, produced by

Pineapple Street Studios, podcast audio, 22:00, https://makinggayhistory
.com/podcast/bonus-episode-from-the-vault-sylvia-rivera-marsha-p-john
son-1970. For additional information about STAR and the history of trans
activism, see Susan Stryker, *Transgender History* (Berkeley, CA: Seal, 2008).

35. Combahee River Collective, "The Combahee River Collective
Statement," April 1977, reprinted by Verso Books Blog, https://www.verso
books.com/blogs/2866-the-combahee-river-collective-statement.

36. Up-to-the-moment information regarding current and future legislation affecting the well-being of trans communities can be found at the
Trans Formations Project, https://www.transformationsproject.org.

37. Heather Love, *Feeling Backward: Loss and the Politics of Queer History* (Cambridge, MA: Harvard University Press, 2007), 2.

38. Love, *Feeling Backward*, 3.

39. Love, 4.

40. Love, 10.

41. R. Kurt Osenlund, "Interview: Alain Guiraudie on *Stranger by the
Lake*."

—⚏—

CONCLUSION

COLLECTIVELY, THE STRATEGIES DISCUSSED IN chapters
3, 4, and 5 provide individual examples of larger trends commonly
seen in queer slashers—that is, slashers written and/or directed
by queer filmmakers. *Serial Mom* (chap. 3) shifts from a queer
killer to a heteronormative killer. *All About Evil* (chap. 4) fosters
queer community through site-specific slasher pastiche. *Stranger
by the Lake* (chap. 5) explores killer queer figures with greater
nuance and empathy. In this conclusion, I want to expand on
these individual examples to show patterns across multiple films.
These three approaches do not account for all methodological approaches taken by queer filmmakers in reimagining the slasher.
However, I hope this language will be useful in describing queer
approaches to the slasher going forward.

Prior studies of queer slashers have focused largely on examples that reproduce the canonical slasher's observed bias toward murdering off the film's most promiscuous and perfunctory
characters. Often with queer stereotypes, such as the gay himbo,
supplanting the heteronormative jock or "meathead." Director
Paul Etheridge's *Hellbent* (2004) has been discussed for its reproduction of the slasher's reactionary traits.[1] The film is set during West Hollywood's Halloween Carnival and follows a group

of gay friends seeking a night of sex and mischief. The protagonist and survivor of the group, Eddie (Dylan Fergus), is its most
competent, thoughtful, and seemingly sexually conservative
(though not unsexual). During an early encounter with the killer
Devil Daddy (a hardbody in a devil mask), the friends expose
their bare asses as a prank, suspecting him to be merely a sexual
voyeur. Eddie is the most reluctant and the last of the group to
comply. The gesture unintentionally arouses the killer's lust/ire,
and those involved become his targets. This construction where
bodily exposure incites murder draws on both the slasher's history of making meathead pranksters into disposable victims and
its trope of voyeuristic arousal ending in death rather than sex.
While *Hellbent* has come to serve as a prototypical queer slasher,
its recommitment to heteronormative ideologies about promiscuity and masculinity makes it a relatively benign reclaiming
of the formula that does not radically reimagine its potential. It
more accurately transplants the slasher to a new locale and friend
group of gay men, offering what a slasher with all its conventions
intact might look like in this new setting.

Scholarly consideration has also been given to the exaggerated
hypermasculinity and flagrant homoeroticism found in the low-
budget horror films of director David DeCoteau.[2] His movies
contain few explicitly gay characters, yet they flaunt hypernormative muscled men's bodies at every turn. This has made him an
object of study as a gay filmmaker straddling an interesting line
between DIY horror and erotic entertainment that sometimes
perplexes a marketplace of unassuming straights who think they
are renting a pure horror title. While his oeuvre spans many horror subgenres, his slasher entries include a trio of early 2000s
slasher-lite films capitalizing on the renewed slasher boom of
the late 1990s—*Final Stab* (2001), *The Frightening* (2002), and
Killer Bash (2005)—and a spate of self-produced slasher hom-
ages distributed digitally by his company Rapid Heart Pictures
such as *1313: Actor Slasher Model* (2011) and *The Brotherhood V:*

Alumni (2009). The latter of these features a rare-for-DeCoteau on-screen gay sex scene. Perhaps DeCoteau's most nuanced take on the queer slasher can be seen in *Killer Bash*. The movie opens with the murder of a college student who is called a "sissy" by his would-be frat brothers during what they describe as a "good old-fashioned geek bashing." Years later, his ghost possesses the body of a young woman and seeks vengeance on the frat's next generation. The film's title hinges on the double meaning of the word *bash* (both a party and an assault), which lends itself easily to the thinly veiled slippage between a *geek bashing* and the more common phrase *gay bashing*. As such, the film plays on the theme of queer trauma leading to violent retribution, which I will discuss as a larger tactic later in this conclusion.

In tandem with this critical evaluation of niche queer slashers, pop culture has properly canonized several queer artists whose work substantively shaped the queer resonances of the mainstream slasher. This has led these artists to speak more publicly about the queer subtext in their work and to explore queer themes further in reiterations of their slasher icons. Don Mancini, who penned all the *Child's Play* movies except the 2016 remake and directed the latter three—*Seed of Chucky* (2004), *Curse of Chucky* (2013), and *Cult of Chucky* (2017)—has revived the killer doll character in the television series *Chucky* (2021–present). Its protagonist, Jake Wheeler (Zackary Arthur), is a fourteen-year-old gay boy who, in the series premiere, watches Chucky murder his homophobic father (Devon Sawa). Mancini told *Out* magazine, "I know as a fourteen-year-old, when I went to see movies like *The Omen* or *Carrie* or *The Fury* . . . where a bullied kid gets supernatural revenge, you know, none of those movies has a single gay character in them. So I think it's good to give kids who are horror fans someone to identify with."[3] Kevin Williamson, screenwriter of *Scream* (Wes Craven, 1996), has also publicly laid claim to the audience-perceived queer subtext of the film's killer duo, Billy (Skeet Ulrich) and Stu (Matthew

Fig 6.1 Stu ignoring Sidney to watch his partner in murder Billy in *Scream* (1996).

Lillard), naming historical queer killers Leopold and Loeb as an inspiration for the pair's dynamic. In a 2022 interview, Williamson remarked, "It's very sort of homoerotic. . . . Is Stu secretly in love with Billy? Maybe. Did Billy manipulate that? Possibly." He continued that at the time he was "very hesitant to present the gay side of me in my work" and that the suffused queerness of killers Billy and Stu was therefore "a little coded and maybe accidental."[4]

I would like to add the below strategies to the collective understanding of how queer filmmakers engage with the slasher's fraught past while also pushing it in new directions. These are not individuated or totalizing strategies. They may coexist within a single film or yield outcomes other than the examples included here. However, these are some of the ways queer filmmakers have seen fit to forge a canon of contemporary queer slashers.

1. SHIFT FROM QUEER KILLER TO HETERONORMATIVE KILLER

Films utilizing this strategy commonly make a transformative change to the slasher formula by disrupting the pattern of associating the killer with queer traits. Instead, the protagonists are often explicitly queer characters under threat of violence by a killer who now represents heteronormative, conservative, and religious ideologies that oppose queer communities. Examples of this include *The Retreat* (Pat Mills, 2021), in which a lesbian couple becomes targeted by a network of homophobic killers who livestream their murders for a hungry digital audience, and *The Ranger* (Jenn Wexler, 2018), about a group of friends fleeing a police raid of a punk bar during which one of them stabbed a cop. The friends are then hunted down by the titular ranger, who writes them up for minor offenses to park etiquette before gruesomely murdering them one by one. These films create queer slashers that do not recommit to the notion that queer people represent a threat to anyone. Rather they acknowledge that queer people are more likely to experience political and legal discrimination as well as outright physical harm. *The Retreat* screenwriter Alyson Richards describes the film as being inspired by an experience when she and her wife felt surveilled and vulnerable during a remote wilderness retreat.[5] The film transforms the slasher's historical uses of voyeurism (most notably, men peering in at women) into a visual style that accentuates queer anxieties about surveillance, often showing us the myriad video screens on which the women are being recorded. Meanwhile, *The Ranger* deliberately invokes the history of countercultural conflicts between marginalized communities and police. By enumerating his victims' trivial infractions against park regulations, the ranger leverages the power of government authority to reclassify his mass murder as the precise eradication of nuisances to the park facade. The use of legal authority, manifested through fussy and improbably shifting restrictions, mirrors real-life tactics by police to strategically set and reset the allowable terms for protest, including the implementation of curfews and other measures to make public existence itself criminal.

2. FOSTER QUEER COMMUNITY THROUGH
SITE-SPECIFIC SLASHER PASTICHE

This refers to communal film projects that utilize existing queer locations and social groups as the backdrop for a slasher. They are often filmed on location in queer venues with local nightlife performers appearing in key roles. While the images on screen depict the killer tearing apart a queer community, the film's production demonstrates a queer community coming together to reflect itself in this easily recognizable film form with a queer past. Often it is through the shared love of the slasher that the community unites, and therefore these films tend to feature significant homage to the subgenre's classics. *Killer Unicorn* (Drew Bolton, 2018) loosely reframes the plot of *I Know What You Did Last Summer* (Jim Gillespie, 1997) as a story of queer peers defending one of their own from sexual violence. When his group of friends discover Danny (Alejandro La Rosa) being sexually assaulted during Brooklyn's biggest annual dance party, they fend off the attacker (who wears a unicorn mask) and believe him to be dead. As the annual nightlife ritual approaches again, the friends find themselves being hunted by the Killer Unicorn, who apparently was not as dead as they thought. A cast of Brooklyn nightlife stars including Biblegirl, Merrie Cherry, and Rify Royalty are featured in key roles. The Spanish film *Cut!* (2021) is modeled more closely after the Italian giallo, with its director, Marc Ferrer, starring as a film director similarly named Marcos. Marcos casts local drag performers from a Barcelona nightclub as the killer's victims in his new giallo film, and they are subsequently murdered in giallo style (using, e.g., first-person camera and gloved hands). Spanish drag queens Marina and La Prohibida appear in these roles. Quickly it becomes clear that Marcos's movie has lethal repercussions as the self-described "meta-cinema" blurs the line between queer Spanish nightlife, Ferrer's movie, and Marcos's diegetic film shoot. These films pay tribute to both the slasher and the respective real-life queer communities in which they are set. They emphasize a whimsical "let's make a movie!" tone that gives off the implication we are watching friends celebrate each other and their local queer scene as much as the horror subgenre they pastiche. Of these three strategies, this one most clearly exemplifies that queer people have seen themselves and want to continue to see themselves in the slasher. Albeit in a manner that reflects the joy and camaraderie of queer communities rather than only treating them as monsters.

3. EXPLORE KILLER QUEER FIGURES WITH GREATER NUANCE AND EMPATHY

While some queer slashers wish to reclaim the slasher to visualize the fun of queer sociality, others choose to lean into the slasher's history of associating queerness with violence. However, these queer-directed slashers more often utilize queer killer characters to dramatize the challenges of everyday queer lives. Queerness is not the cause of the killer impulse in these films. Violence more often comes from queer trauma and a history of abuse. *Knife+Heart* (Yann Gonzalez, 2018) features a masked killer, Guy (Jonathan Genet), who was castrated and left for dead by his father upon discovering a queer relationship between Guy and another boy at fifteen. Guy then sets out to murder the actors and the director, Anne (Vanessa Paradis), of a gay porno. Ultimately, we learn the connection between Guy and Anne is that she made a film with a scenario similar to his lived tragedy, where a father stumbled onto two boys having sex, with the decidedly more erotic outcome of a group sex scene. *Knife+Heart* concludes with emotional crosscutting between Anne's erotic film and a flashback to Guy being attacked, contrasting the potentiality of queer fantasy and the reality of queer trauma. *Bad Girl Boogey* (2022) identifies itself in its opening titles as "a transgender and queer film by Alice Maio Mackay." Here, director

Mackay uses the motif of the masked killer as an allegory for the intervention that she as a trans filmmaker is making into the slasher itself. In her film, the mask that the killer wears dates back to Germany's Weimar period and is linked to Nazism and other forms of malignant bigotry and violent persecution. Notably, it is clarified that the mask does not possess its wearer but "frees" them and allows them to express their already existing hatred. This purposefully undermines the potential to defer blame for the legacy of antiqueer violence associated with the mask. It also accepts the potential for transformation by seeing the mask not as a static antiqueer force but as a conduit for violent expressions of anger. We see this when Clive (Lewi Dawson) dons the mask and uses its powers to strangle Chase (Toshiro Glenn), the school homophobe who calls the film's central queer friend group "faggots." The act allegorizes Alice Maio Mackay's own recalibration of the slasher (as embodied in the mask) to express rage against oppressive forces of antiqueer violence. She says that the film "takes the slasher out of the hands of the Reaganite '80s mentality of punishment and violence and turns it into a powerful and resonant allegory for the struggles of the LGBTQ+ community, and all of those who are hated and outcast."[6] Examples such as these use cinematic violence to express complex feelings of rage and trauma associated with tangible anti-queer harm. They do not rebuke queer relationships with violence in the slasher but instead see the killer queer as a conduit they may grab control of in order to achieve queer aims.

A queer slasher is a film made by queer filmmakers that engages with a film form known historically as one that villainizes queer and trans people. It is the working of a cinematic wound, a reclaiming of a term of injury. A redeployment of language used against us to phrase our own identities within the system of filmic language we have inherited. Perhaps with the hope that we might change the meanings of this language, or at least achieve some

Fig 6.2 Following her performance as the killer in her gay porno, Anne in *Knife+Heart* (2018) asks the question that we all ask of ourselves from time to time: "Was I a good fag?"

control within it. That the antiqueer perspectives that forged Norman Bates and Freddy Krueger might give way to something new. Like John Waters's brazen and unapologetic star turns for beautiful filth queen Divine. Or his gloating, untouchably "normal" suburban killer Beverly Sutphin. Joshua Grannell's movie maven turned menacing killer Deborah Tennis, or his gore-couture adorned stage and screen persona Peaches Christ. The scary and sexy Michel of Alain Guiraudie's *Stranger by the Lake* (2013). The "geek-bashed" nerd who annihilates the alpha muscle bros who murdered him in *Killer Bash* (2005). The eroticized Devil Daddy who haunts the sexual meat market of West Hollywood in *Hellbent* (2004). A man in a rainbow unicorn mask with unfinished business at Brooklyn's Annual Enema Party Where You Come Get Douched and Dance in *Killer Unicorn* (2018). Lesbians joining together fighting for their lives against bigots in *The Retreat* (2021). Punks rejecting abusive authority in *The Ranger* (2018). Queer and trans teens battling their bullies in *Bad Girl Boogey* (2022). In the absence of the ability to "undo" a cultural and cinematic history associating queerness with killer violence, queer filmmakers instead remake the slasher in their own image.

NOTES

1. See Darren Elliott-Smith's chapter "Gay Slasher Horror: Devil Daddies and Final Boys," in *Queer Horror Film and Television: Sexuality and Masculinity at the Margins* (London: I. B. Taurus, 2016); and Claire Sisco King, "Un-Queering Horror: *Hellbent* and the Policing of the 'Gay Slasher,'" *Western Journal of Communication* 74, no. 3 (2010): 249–68.

2. See Darren Elliott-Smith's chapter "The Rise of Queer Fear: De-Coteau and Gaysploitation Horror," in *Queer Horror Film and Television: Sexuality and Masculinity at the Margins* (London: I. B. Taurus, 2016); and Harry Benshoff's chapter "'Way Too Gay to Be Ignored': The Production and Reception of Queer Horror Cinema in the Twenty-First Century," in *Speaking of Monsters: A Teratological Anthology*, eds. Caroline Joan S. Picart and John Edgar Browning (New York: Palgrave MacMillan, 2012).

3. Donald Padgett, "Chucky Is Back & Queerer Than Ever Thanks to His Gay Creator," *Out*, October 12, 2021, https://www.out.com/print /2021/10/12/chucky-back-queerer-ever-thanks-his-gay-creator.

4. Chris Azzopardi, "'Scream' Screenwriter Kevin Williamson Confirms Billy and Stu's Queer-Coded Relationship Was Based on Real Gay Killers," last updated January 12, 2022, https://pridesource.com/article /billyandstu.

5. Josh Millican, "Trailer: Queer Horror THE RETREAT Now Set for May 21st Release," *Dread Central*, last updated April 21, 2021, https:// www.dreadcentral.com/news/393037/trailer-queer-horror-the-retreat-now -set-for-may-21st-release.

6. John Squire, "'Bad Girl Boogey'—Transgender Filmmaker Alice Maio Mackay Announces Queer Slasher Movie," Bloody Disgusting, last updated February 21, 2022, https://bloody-disgusting.com/movie /3704378/bad-girl-boogey-transgender-filmmaker-alice-maio-mackay -announces-queer-slasher-movie.

FILMOGRAPHY FOR FURTHER CONSIDERATION

THIS IS A LIST OF slasher-related features written and/or directed by queer filmmakers that have not been significantly discussed in the chapters of this book. I include this to acknowledge the work of more queer artists in forging new versions of the slasher and in hopes it helps us to continue conversations about queer slashers in both popular and academic contexts. As a community, we have seen ourselves in queer traces within mainstream horror, such as Don Mancini's Chucky, Kevin Williamson's Ghostface, or Mark Patton's Jesse. However, queer audiences might be better served by fostering our own canon of queer slashers. We might choose instead to celebrate *Hellbent*'s Devil Daddy or the *Killer Unicorn*. *Death Drop Gorgeous*'s fading queen Gloria Hole or vital horror queen Vivika Darko as a new queer-authored nightmare killer a la Freddy Krueger in *Please Don't Make Me*. In a universalizing sense, queerness abounds in the slasher. But in a minoritizing sense, these are our slashers.

Psycho Beach Party (Robert Lee King, 2000)
I'll Bury You Tomorrow (Alan Rowe Kelly, 2002)
Make a Wish (Sharon Ferranti, 2002)
Dead Boyz Don't Scream (Marc Saltarelli, 2006)
The Blood Shed (Alan Rowe Kelly, 2007)

Fraternity Massacre at Hell Island (Mark Jones, 2007)
The Gay Bed & Breakfast of Terror (Jaymes Thompson, 2007)
Fright Flick (Israel Luna, 2011)
Scary Larry (Todd Nunes, 2012)
Bloody Homecoming (Brian C. Weed, 2013)
Varsity Blood (Jake Helgren, 2014)
All Through the House (Todd Nunes, 2015)
The Final Girls (Todd Strauss-Schulson, 2015)
You're Killing Me (Jim Hansen, 2015)
Better Watch Out (Chris Peckover, 2016)
Pitchfork (Glenn Douglas Packard, 2016)
Alpha Delta Zatan (Art Arutyunyan, 2017)
B&B (Joe Ahearne, 2017)
Bear Creek (George Climer, 2017)
The Getaway (Henderson Maddox, 2017)
Happy Death Day (Christopher Landon, 2017)
Party Night (Troy Escamilla, 2017)
Devil's Path (Matthew Montgomery, 2018)
Mrs. Claus (Troy Escamilla, 2018)
All That We Destroy (Chelsea Stardust, 2019)
Blind (Marcel Walz, 2019)
Camp Wedding (Greg Emetaz, 2019)
Last Ferry (Jaki Bradley, 2019)
Midnight Kiss (Carter Smith, 2019)
Cuties (Joshua Gratton, 2020)
Death Drop Gorgeous (Michael J. Ahern, Christopher Dalpe, and Brandon
    Perras, 2020)
Freaky (Christopher Landon, 2020)
Initiation (John Berardo, 2020)
The Last Thanksgiving (Erick Lorinc, 2020)
Teacher Shortage (Troy Escamilla, 2020)
The Fear Street Trilogy (Leigh Janiak, 2021)
Pretty Boy (Marcel Walz, 2021)
Bitch Ass (Bill Posley, 2022)
The Blackening (Tim Story, 2022)
Children of Sin (Christopher Wesley Moore, 2022)
Please Don't Make Me (Vivika Darko/Canaan White, 2022)
Sick (John Hyams, 2022)
The Latent Image (Alexander Birrell, 2022)
They/Them (John Logan, 2022)

The Bell Keeper (Colton Tran, 2023)
Departing Seniors (Clare Cooney, 2023)
It's A Wonderful Knife (Tyler MacIntyre, 2023)
LGBT: Lethal Gay Butcher of Terror (Tyler Thomas, 2023)
The Sacrifice Game (Jenn Wexler, 2023)
Sorry, Charlie (Colton Tran, 2023)
That's a Wrap (Marcel Walz, 2023)
Totally Killer (Nahnatchka Khan, 2023)
When the Trash Man Knocks (Christopher Wesley Moore, 2023)

BIBLIOGRAPHY

Althusser, Louis. *Lenin and Philosophy, and Other Essays*. New York: Monthly Review, 2001.

Armstrong, Kent Byron. *Slasher Films: An International Filmography, 1960 through 2001*. Jefferson, NC: McFarland, 2003.

Benshoff, Harry. *Monsters in the Closet: Homosexuality and the Horror Film*. Manchester, UK: Manchester University Press, 1997.

———. "'Way Too Gay to Be Ignored': The Production and Reception of Queer Horror Cinema in the Twenty-First Century." In *Speaking of Monsters: A Teratological Anthology*, edited by Caroline Joan S. Picart and John Edgar Browning, 131–44. New York: Palgrave MacMillan, 2012.

Berlant, Lauren, and Michael Warner. "Sex in Public." *Critical Inquiry* 24, no. 2 (winter 1998): 547–66.

Bersani, Leo. *Homos*. Cambridge, MA: Harvard University Press, 1995.

———. *Is the Rectum a Grave? And Other Essays*. Chicago: University of Chicago Press, 2010.

Bérubé, Allan. *Coming Out under Fire: The History of Gay Men and Women in World War Two*. New York: Free Press, 1990.

Butler, Judith. *Bodies That Matter: On the Discursive Limits of Sex*. New York: Routledge, 1993.

Chauncey, George. *Gay New York: Gender, Urban Culture, and the Makings of the Gay Male World, 1890–1940*. New York: Basic, 1994.

Clover, Carol J. *Men, Women, and Chain Saws: Gender in the Modern Horror Film*. Princeton, NJ: Princeton University Press, 1992.

Cohen, Cathy J. "Punks, Bulldaggers, and Welfare Queens: The Radical Potential of Queer Politics?" In *Sexual Identities, Queer Politics*, edited by Mark Blasius, 200–28. Princeton, NJ: Princeton University Press, 2001.

D' Emilio, John. *Sexual Politics, Sexual Communities: The Making of a Homosexual Minority in the United States, 1940–1970*. Chicago: University of Chicago, 1983.

Dika, Vera. *Games of Terror: Halloween, Friday the 13th, and the Films of the Stalker Cycle*. Madison, NJ: Farleigh Dickenson University Press, 1990.

Doty, Alexander. *Making Things Perfectly Queer: Interpreting Mass Culture*. Minneapolis: University of Minnesota Press, 1993.

Duggan, Lisa. *The Twilight of Equality? Neoliberalism, Cultural Politics, and the Attack on Democracy*. Boston: Beacon, 2014.

Dyer, Richard. *Pastiche*. New York: Routledge, 2007.

Edelman, Lee. *No Future: Queer Theory and the Death Drive*. Durham, NC: Duke University Press, 2004.

Elliott-Smith, Darren. *Queer Horror Film and Television: Sexuality and Masculinity at the Margins*. London: I. B. Tauris, 2016.

Elliott-Smith, Darren, and John Edgar Browning, eds. *New Queer Horror Film and Television*. Cardiff, UK: University of Wales Press, 2021.

Foucault, Michel. *The History of Sexuality, Volume 1: An Introduction*. Translated by Robert Hurley. New York: Vintage, 1990.

Frank, Gillian. "'The Civil Rights of Parents': Race and Conservative Politics in Anita Bryant's Campaign Against Gay Rights in 1970s Florida." *Journal of the History of Sexuality* 22, no. 1 (January 2013): 126–60.

Goltz, Dustin Bradley. *Queer Temporalities in Gay Male Representation: Tragedy, Normativity, and Futurity*. London: Routledge, 2011.

Halberstam, Jack. *Skin Shows: Gothic Horror and the Technology of Monsters*. Durham, NC: Duke University Press, 1995.

Hay, Harry. *Radically Gay: Gay Liberation in the Words of Its Founder*. Boston: Beacon, 2001.

Katz, Jonathan Ned. *Gay American History: Lesbians and Gay Men in the U.S.A.* New York: Meridian, 1992.

King, Claire Sisco. "Un-Queering Horror: *Hellbent* and the Policing of the 'Gay Slasher.'" *Western Journal of Communication* 74, no. 3 (2010): 249–68.

Lassiter, Matthew D. *The Silent Majority: Suburban Politics in the Sunbelt South*. Princeton, NJ: Princeton University Press, 2006.

Lorde, Audre. *Sister Outsider: Essays and Speeches*. Berkeley, CA: Crossing Press, 2015.

Loudermilk, A. "Last to Leave the Theater: Sissy Spectatorship of Stalker Movies and the 'Final Girls' Who Survive Them." *Bright Lights Film*

Journal (October 2012). http://brightlightsfilm.com/last-to-leave-the
-theater-sissy-spectatorship-of-stalker-movies-and-the-final-girls-who
-survive-them#.WwRbs-4vzcs.

Love, Heather. *Feeling Backward: Loss and the Politics of Queer History.*
Cambridge, MA: Harvard University Press, 2009.

Mank, Gregory. *Laird Cregar: A Hollywood Tragedy.* Jefferson, NC:
McFarland, 2019.

McCarty, John. *Movie Psychos and Madmen: Film Psychopaths from Jekyll
and Hyde to Hannibal Lecter.* New York: Citadel, 1993.

———. *Splatter Movies: Breaking the Last Taboo of the Screen.* New York:
St. Martin's, 1984.

Meyerowitz, Joanne. "Transforming Sex: Christine Jorgensen in the Postwar U.S." *Magazine of History* 20, no.2 (2006): 16–20.

Moon, Michael. *A Small Boy and Others: Imitation and Initiation in American Culture from Henry James to Andy Warhol.* Durham, NC: Duke
University Press, 1998.

Muñoz, José Esteban. *Cruising Utopia: The Then and There of Queer Futurity.* New York: NYU Press, 2009.

Ngai, Sianne. *Theory of the Gimmick: Aesthetic Judgment and Capitalist
Form.* Cambridge, MA: Harvard University Press, 2020.

Nowell, Richard. *Blood Money: A History of the First Teen Slasher Film
Cycle.* New York: Continuum, 2010.

Olivier, Marc. "Gidget Goes Noir: William Castle and the Teenage Phone
Fatale." *Journal of Popular Film and Television* 41, no. 1 (2013): 31–42.

Owens, Andrew J. *Desire after Dark: Contemporary Queer Cultures and
Occultly Marvelous Media.* Bloomington: Indiana University Press,
2021.

Pinedo, Isabel Cristina. *Recreational Terror: Women and the Pleasures of
Horror Film Viewing.* Albany: State University of New York Press, 1997.

Rich, B. Ruby. *New Queer Cinema: The Director's Cut.* Durham, NC: Duke
University Press, 2013.

Roberts, Nicole E. "The Plight of Gay Visibility: Intolerance in San Francisco, 1970–1979." *Journal of Homosexuality* 60, no. 1 (2013): 105–19.

Rockoff, Adam. *Going to Pieces: The Rise and Fall of the Slasher Film,
1978–1986.* Jefferson, NC: McFarland, 2011.

Sanjek, David. "The Doll and the Whip: Pathos and Ballyhoo in William
Castle's *Homicidal.*" *Quarterly Review of Film and Video* 20, no. 4 (2003):
247–63.

Schechter, Harold. *Deviant: The Shocking True Story of Ed Gein, the Original Psycho.* New York: Pocket Books, 1999.

Schoell, William. *Stay Out of the Shower: 25 Years of Shocker Films Beginning with "Psycho."* New York: Dembner, 1985.

Sedgwick, Eve Kosofsky. *Epistemology of the Closet.* Berkeley: University of California Press, 1990.

———. *Tendencies.* Durham, NC: Duke University Press, 1993.

———. *Touching Feeling: Affect, Pedagogy, Performativity.* Durham, NC: Duke University Press, 2006.

Shouse, Eric. "Feeling, Emotion, Affect." *M/C Journal* 8, no. 6 (2005).

Smith, Angela M. *Hideous Progeny: Disability, Eugenics, and Classic Horror Cinema.* New York: Columbia University Press, 2012.

Smith, Murray. "Gangsters, Cannibals, Aesthetes, or Apparently Perverse Allegiances." In *Passionate Views: Film, Cognition, and Emotion,* edited by Carl Plantinga and Greg M. Smith, 217–38. Baltimore, MD: John Hopkins University Press, 1999.

Staiger, Janet. *Perverse Spectators: The Practices of Film Reception.* New York: New York University Press, 2000.

Stevenson, Jack. "From the Bedroom to the Bijou: A Secret History of Gay American Sex Cinema." *Film Quarterly* 51, no. 1 (fall 1997): 24–31.

Sullivan, K. E. "Ed Gein and the Figure of the Transgender Serial Killer." *Jump Cut* 43 (2000): 38–47.

Tudor, Andrew. *Monsters and Mad Scientists: A Cultural History of the Horror Movie.* Oxford, UK: Basil Blackwell, 1989.

Wahlert, Lance. "The Burden of Poofs: Criminal Pathology, Clinical Scrutiny, and Queer Etiology in Queer Cinema." *Journal of Medical Humanities* 34 (March 2013): 149–75.

Warner, Michael "Introduction." In *Fear of a Queer Planet: Queer Politics and Social Theory,* edited by Michael Warner, vii-xxxi. Minneapolis: University of Minnesota Press, 1993.

Waters, John. *Crackpot: The Obsessions of John Waters.* London: Scribner, 2003.

———. *Shock Value: A Tasteful Book about Bad Taste.* London: Running Press, 2005.

Williams, Linda. "When the Woman Looks." In *The Dread of Difference: Gender and the Horror Film,* edited by Barry Keith Grant, 15–34. Austin: University of Texas Press, 1996.

Wood, Robin. *Hollywood from Vietnam to Reagan.* New York: Columbia University Press, 1986.

Worland, Rick. *The Horror Film: An Introduction.* Malden, MA: Blackwell, 2007.

INDEX

PETER MARRA is Assistant Professor of Teaching in English and Gender, Sexuality, and Women's Studies at Wayne State University.

For Indiana University Press

Tony Brewer, *Artist and Book Designer*
Allison Chaplin, *Acquisitions Editor*
Anna Garnai, *Editorial Assistant*
Sophia Hebert, *Assistant Acquisitions Editor*
Samantha Heffner, *Marketing and Publicity Manager*
Brenna Hosman, *Production Coordinator*
Katie Huggins, *Production Manager*
David Miller, *Lead Project Manager/Editor*
Dan Pyle, *Online Publishing Manager*
Jennifer Witzke, *Senior Artist and Book Designer*